T0268284

EVERYONE AGAINST US

CHICAGO VISIONS AND REVISIONS

Edited by Matthew Briones, Melanie Newport, Carlo Rotella,
Bill Savage, and Robert Stepto

ALSO IN THE SERIES:

The Blues Dream of Billy Boy Arnold
BY BILLY BOY ARNOLD WITH KIM FIELD

Never a City So Real: A Walk in Chicago
BY ALEX KOTLOWITZ

*The World Is Always Coming to an End: Pulling Together
and Apart in a Chicago Neighborhood*
BY CARLO ROTELLA

Bitten by the Blues: The Alligator Records Story
BY BRUCE IGLAUER AND PATRICK A. ROBERTS

Dirty Waters: Confessions of Chicago's Last Harbor Boss
BY R. J. NELSON

Friends Disappear: The Battle for Racial Equality in Evanston
BY MARY BARR

You Were Never in Chicago
BY NEIL STEINBERG

Hack: Stories from a Chicago Cab
BY DMITRY SAMAROV

The Third City: Chicago and American Urbanism
BY LARRY BENNETT

The Wagon and Other Stories from the City
BY MARTIN PREIB

Soldier Field: A Stadium and Its City
BY LIAM T. A. FORD

*The Plan of Chicago: Daniel Burnham and the Remaking
of the American City*
BY CARL SMITH

EVERYONE AGAINST US

PUBLIC DEFENDERS AND THE
MAKING OF AMERICAN JUSTICE

ALLEN GOODMAN

The University of Chicago Press

Chicago and London

The University of Chicago Press, Chicago 60637
The University of Chicago Press, Ltd., London
Published 2023
Printed in the United States of America

32 31 30 29 28 27 26 25 24 23   1 2 3 4 5

ISBN-13: 978-0-226-82623-3 (cloth)
ISBN-13: 978-0-226-82624-0 (e-book)
DOI: https://doi.org/10.7208/
chicago/9780226826240.001.0001

Library of Congress Cataloging-in-Publication Data

Names: Goodman, Allen, author.
Title: Everyone against us : public defenders and the making of
American justice / Allen Goodman.
Other titles: Chicago visions + revisions.
Description: Chicago : The University of Chicago Press, 2023. |
Series: Chicago visions and revisions | Includes bibliographical
references and index.
Identifiers: LCCN 2022042511 | ISBN 9780226826233 (cloth) |
ISBN 9780226826240 (ebook)
Subjects: LCSH: Goodman, Allen. | Public defenders—Illinois—
Cook County—Biography. | Criminal justice, Administration of—
Illinois—Cook County.
Classification: LCC KF373.G6195 A3 2023 |
DDC 340.0922773/1—dc23/eng/20221101
LC record available at https://lccn.loc.gov/2022042511

♾ This paper meets the requirements of
ANSI/NISO Z39.48-1992 (Permanence of Paper).

With my eternal love for Ilona, my guardian angel,
and our beautiful children, Jacob and Mayah

CONTENTS

PREFACE

"Criminal justice" isn't a particularly warm term, but it's doing a lot of work.

Those two words are standing for all of the philosophies, politics, procedures, and punishments that comprise an official system of making formal accusations of specific types of public harm; constructing a suitably reliable and fair process of proof; imposing sanctions to strip away property, liberty, and possibly even life itself; and, ideally, performing all the attendant practicalities while believing in, and persuading the masses of, the substantial righteousness of the outcomes. Even for a legal or philosophical construct, that's some pretty heavy lifting.

Given the evolution of technology, changing sensibilities and norms, and, perhaps most importantly, natural career turnover of the individuals who make legislation, run prosecutorial offices, and serve as enforcement officers, criminal justice systems of a given place have loosely defined eras, almost like generations. The eras flow into and out of one another, forming a stream of influence that leaves stains of its high- and low-water marks of nobility and ignominy, inevitably containing some stones of precedent that stand strong despite the force of erosion in the movement. Traces of the past may be faint like a faded fossil; others redirect the river altogether.

This book is a collection of professional and personal experiences and perspectives that are centered on and related to my work as an assistant public defender (APD) in Cook County, Illinois, the dominant part of which is the city of Chicago. APDs are government-employed criminal defense lawyers, appointed by the court as a matter of American constitutional rights to represent people who cannot afford to retain private counsel. From 1996 to 2004, I was part of the Public Defender's Office, first as an intern, then as a licensed student practitioner, and finally as a staff attorney. For approximately six of those nine years, I was assigned to the Felony Trial Division. Although the principal place of my assignment was the suburban District 2 courthouse in Skokie, four courtrooms there were exclusively dedicated to cases from Chicago Police districts on the North and West Sides of the city, and I worked in one of those.

In telling these stories, I have tried to be accurate, insightful, reasonable in my conclusions and advocacy, and compelling, all while respecting the confines of my former clients' rights. As a defense attorney, I certainly realize and concede that the extent to which I've succeeded or failed in any of those measures is ultimately for others to judge. My humble hope is that when you read what I have written, you will grant me the latitude of fair consideration, even if you don't agree with all of it as a matter of fact, discretion, or principle.

I should warn you, some of this stuff is pretty dark.

There are passages about physical violence including sexual crimes against children and adults, homicidal and grossly injurious acts, desecration of corpses, prisoner abuse, behavioral depravity, desperation, and death. There are also passages about systemic violence in the forms of false convictions, racism, and other types of prejudice, some of which contain quotations of explicitly racist language. These stories are not intended to be entirely comfortable to read, but illustrate the stakes of criminal justice for the human beings involved. In recalling and describing the collective weight and discomfort of these events, I was mentally processing them as interpersonal experiences, either for me or for the individual participants. For me, and for many other workers in the criminal justice systems of the world, violence isn't abstract or theoretical; it needs to be handled professionally and understood as an element in a day's work in societal governance. But it certainly takes a toll, and that's definitely part of the reason why I've written this book. If it's hard to read, it was perhaps even harder to witness and address.

Given the inherent themes of race and racism in describing an era that was "the high point of mass incarceration in Cook County," with an estimated 90 percent of the more than 100,000 people a year who went to Cook County Jail at that time being racial minorities, it's been suggested that I should address my participation in that enterprise in light of my "whiteness." It's a fair question for anyone to pose, and a perfect opportunity to provide a lawyer's favorite answer: it's complicated.

My skin is white, but I am a Jew. None of the people or institutions whose interest is to ascribe supremacy or even membership to an in-group based on race would ever accept me as white. People may take a look at me and presume privilege, but I get few of the actual benefits. Actually, I don't get recognized either way; as David Baddiel so powerfully describes in his book *Jews Don't Count*, Jews are only 2.4 percent of the American population, and yet are never recognized as having minority status for any of the measures that claim to determine exactly such things. Without trying to write a book that is fundamentally about me, I hope the point comes through the entire work that I identify far more with American underclasses than I ever could with white European American conservatives.

Along those lines, during the time I was an APD, I was known as Allen Gutterman, which was the family name of my adoptive parents. Gutterman is a transliteration of the Yiddish for "good man." However, most people aren't that familiar with Yiddish, and obviously the English meaning of Gutterman isn't the same, practically reversing the original intent with a particular urban slant. I can assure you from personal experience that Jews growing up in America with the name Gutterman do not get all the benefits of white privilege, unless those benefits include being teased, mocked, and bullied throughout most of their lives.

True story: Having endured every conceivable variation and disrespect on my name from elementary school through university, I figured that attaining the status of lawyer would finally provide me some mature refuge from that crap. For the most part it did; with only rare, occasional exceptions, I made it through all my years of law school and as a public defender without being openly ridiculed for my name. When I achieved enough litigation success to be recruited from the PD's Office to one of Chicago's most prestigious private law firms, I was even more optimistic that my days of harassment were permanently over. Until one day I was asked to be on a phone call with a very senior partner of the firm and an extremely senior executive of a German company. When I was introduced, the German executive asked the partner to clarify the pronunciation of my name. While I listened silently, the partner explained that although the usual way of saying it was exactly as he'd heard it, if he would be more comfortable, he could feel free to change it and call me "Güterman," to which the executive replied, "Yes, that's much more elegant, I think I will." I guess I shouldn't have been too surprised, considering some of the people with whom I was working. That same partner had been a federal prosecutor before moving to private practice, and there was always a rumor that both state and federal prosecutors have an unwritten rule to always wear white dress shirts. In trying to dress the part of a successful attorney, I'd bought myself a few pastel shirts to mix and match with various neckties and suits, to keep my daily wardrobe fresh. He took me aside one day as we were about to get into an elevator and asked me about my sartorial choices. When I told him that I was just trying to avoid being boring, he locked me in a glare of gleeful condescension, giving me the sense that he was perfectly pleased with his double entendre, and said in his trademark near-whisper: "White is the only color with credibility."

A lot of politics and law happen behind closed doors, even though both democracy and justice are premised on public transparency. The tension between getting things done and getting things done the right way will probably persist forever, and good people will have to make tough choices. I remember the last time that I was able to state on the record: "Assistant Public Defender Allen Gutterman, for the defendant." As I wrote in my letter of resignation, it was my honor to serve the people and the ideals we represent. Having stopped practicing in the courts of Illinois, at least I can continue in the court of public opinion, trying to shed light on my era of criminal justice in Chicago.

So for this new record, it's just Allen Goodman for the public, but I hope I remain a defender forever.

I. JAIL RULES

Chicago's central criminal court and jail complex aren't operated by the city government. In Illinois, local courts and jails are run by county authorities, and although Chicago is Illinois's biggest and most famous city by far, it's just one of over 130 municipalities and unincorporated areas that form Cook County. The courthouse and jail buildings are located a few miles away from downtown, on the Southwest Side of the city. They occupy a sprawling campus that's anchored at the intersection of 26th Street and California Avenue, so most of the people who work in Chicago's criminal justice system refer to the epicenter of that world as "26th and Cal."

The Cook County Jail (officially the Department of Corrections) is the central jail for the entire Chicago metropolitan area. The vast majority of the people who are held there were arrested somewhere else and were processed through local police stations before they arrived at the county lockup, so the initial shock of their arrests has usually worn off before they get there. They are shipped to 26th and Cal for bond court, a discordant daily ritual involving a literal parade of arrestees put through very brief and perfunctory court appearances that establish the monetary cost of their temporary freedom in the form of bail.

The bond court holding pens are directly beneath the large first-floor courtroom where those hearings occur on a daily basis. As a

lawyer there to represent the accused, access to the holding pens and
the clients requires us to pass through the courtroom into a sort of
backstage hallway leading to a narrow set of stairs that descend into
a labyrinthine alternative reality containing an absurd and volatile
mix of humanity. Before we can see the lockup, we can smell it; the
whole place is simmered in the rank atmosphere of a convection
oven of stench. On any given morning, the pens are an overcrowded,
unventilated concentration of over a hundred unshowered detainees
who are radiating a combination of multicultural musk and whatever
soaked into yesterday's clothes. Inevitably, some have no choice but
to use the common commodes in plain view of everyone there. In addition to the hygienic challenges, the "guests" are an emotional mix
of the sleepy, hungover, strung-out, pissed-off, scared, and mentally
ill. Nevertheless, bond hearings offer a moment of hope for the prisoners, all but the worst of whom are interested in the active process
that might see them released, or will at least provide some answers
about their situations and their immediate futures.

   On one Christmas morning in the early 2000s, I was a young assistant Cook County public defender working beneath Chicago's
central criminal court in the massive holding pens full of people who
had been arrested on Christmas Eve. My assignment was to process
individuals for Holiday Bond Court, the special session that occurs
based on laws that require the government to give people due process without delay, even on public holidays. There were four or five
of us PDs working the holiday for overtime pay, and we each had a
clipboard full of single-page form questionnaires to document some
personal information about our insta-clients.

   We would walk up to the bars and call out a list of names so that
the prisoners could line up for processing. Our fact-gathering required a fine balance of professionalism and speed; about half of the
questions on each form were skipped or triaged due to a combination
of time constraints, the rapid-fire rhythm of the hearings, the relatively straightforward life experiences of the majority of the people

we were meeting, and a strategic desire to avoid bad news. Frankly, most people in jail settings are kind of used to it. The people who work there function on routine, and a significant number of the inmates are the type the staff calls "frequent fliers." Most of the charges were standard drunk-tank fare, such as disorderly conduct, simple drug possession, trespassing, and thefts. Owing to the season, there was a slightly above-average percentage of retail theft and simple battery. Charges like drunk driving and domestic violence went to other courthouses, so none of that. A few felonies sprinkled in were more serious charges, but we faced no major headline cases or extreme violence of the kind that would put people on edge.

Christmas in jail is better than jail on most other days: the dangerous and depressing elements don't disappear, but there is an atmosphere of joviality and mercy that is normally sorely lacking. There tend to be more family visits, more interactions with counselors and various volunteers, and slightly better meals. Still, holiday moods among the staff in criminal court have a weird way of spiking to either end of the spectrum. Some people find an extra measure of compassion, while others can literally twitch with aggravation. Whatever the layers of emotion are for each individual, there's an unspoken but palpable agreement that nobody really wants to be there. Accordingly, there is pressure on the courtroom personnel to get the court call done as fast as possible—which is the standard attitude anyway—but it's especially pronounced for Holiday Bond Court, since the workers and at least some of the detainees know that freedom awaits them at the end of the proceedings.

Probably everyone has experienced frustration at one time or another with people failing to follow basic instructions, but the setting we were in created an overflow of tension for one of the sheriff's deputies that morning. At his personal intersection of responsibility and power, there was a combustible mix of holiday pressure to finish work and go home, slapdash paperwork, a security tinderbox, and his self-righteous superiority over the defendants, whom the sheriffs routinely deride as "mopes." I'm sure the stink didn't help either. He was trying to give some instructions to the detainees in order to move the group along, but they did not exemplify military precision in their attention, retention, or movements. He started screaming: *"Listen up! Since none of you mopes can follow simple instructions, we're gonna do a little exercise!"* He had a real directive anger in his voice. At first he didn't care that there were several defense attorneys right in front of him, but when our frightened faces registered our objections to his power trip and his interference with us doing our jobs, he just ordered us out of the lockup. We moved quickly, because one of the sanctified rules of working in the jail is that it is the sheriff's house, where deference to their instructions is nearly absolute.

We could hear the rest of it from around the corner, out of sight but certainly not out of earshot. *"Get up! Get up! All you mother-fuckers stand the fuck up! Nobody sittin' on the benches! Up on your toes, you fuckin' mopes, get up! We're going to do some squats to wake everybody up! Keep going 'til I say stop! One! Two! Three!"* Stress positions aren't really a part of everyday conversation, but the term got some traction in American media outlets around the time that US soldiers were being accused of mistreatment and torture of prisoners at Abu Ghraib during the second Iraq War. Ethical use of force is a complicated academic topic, with inevitable disagreements even among experts. Actual use of force is much simpler. Mandatory exercise is a time-tested jail favorite because the officers don't have to actually touch anyone while they do it. It can be easily denied for lack of proof. And if denial fails, it can be claimed as a health benefit despite being used as a punishment. The best cruelties not only inflict pain in the moment, but set up the victims for a twist of gaslighting too, in case the abused dare complain.

I wasn't the lead PD there that day; someone who had been in the office for many more years than I had—and thus was much higher on the seniority, responsibility, and pay scales—was in that role. We huddled quickly as a group to discuss the situation. Whether to complain or not sounds simple in the abstract, but it's not that easy in practice. Formal accusations of mistreatment would be a serious issue and are guaranteed to make an enemy out of a key deputy or crew with the power to exact plenty of revenge on the prisoners when we're gone. They can also make our jobs a lot tougher by limiting or denying our access to the people we need to represent. Even those of us who hadn't seen that type of behavior before realized quite quickly that the deputy's willingness to flex right in front of PDs contained a message to us too.

Being a public defender is different from being a private defense attorney for many reasons, but maybe the biggest difference is that we are part of "the system," and privates are not. We have to be there every day, assigned in long rotations to a particular division and courtroom. As a PD, you can make an issue out of whatever you observe in the jails, knowing that the overwhelmingly likely outcome of such a course of action will only be some form of retaliation, or you can try to understand the situation in the context of order and discipline, wait it out for a few minutes, and get back to work. Besides, there are several ways to register an objection that are less formal and might even be more effective because they are much more immediate. Our senior PD found a "white shirt," one of the sergeants who are the first-line supervisors of the regular deputies who wear blue, and basically said something along the lines of "What the fuck?" The sergeant probably didn't spend much mental energy on the question of whether or not his deputy was abusing prisoners or on considerations of what the group of lawyers who were witnessing it might do about it, but he certainly understood that these shenanigans were wasting time. He went around the corner: *"That's enough! The judge'll be on the bench in five minutes."*

Holidays weren't the only time I witnessed such raw behaviors in the jail. A few years later, I was assigned to work with a veteran judge who had a long-standing reputation as a tough sentencer, what the old-timers called a "banger" before that word was repurposed for gang members. I regularly appeared on that judge's call because my bosses knew that I had earned his respect the hard way: he and I had gotten off to a horrible start very early in my career when he accused me of trying to pull a speedy trial scam that I didn't even know existed.

Speedy trial rules are imposed both by the Constitution and by statute; they require the prosecution to move cases forward in a timely manner at each stage of the proceedings. The ultimate underlying purpose is to allow people to demand a speedy trial with minimal delays, as a way of preventing them from spending too much time locked up and facing serious legal and personal jeopardy if they turn out to be innocent. The amount of time that the State has to bring a case to trial is called the "term." Managing the term is a critical practical lesson that isn't taught in law school, and it's the reason that every single continuance granted in Chicago criminal court is officially recorded as being allowed as a result of "Motion State," "Motion Defendant," or the most common, "By Agreement." Motion State continuances run the speedy trial clock, whereas the other two don't count against the term. Violations of those rules carry the possible penalty of dismissing the relevant case, and assistant state's attorneys (ASAs) who "blow the term" are not-so-gently encouraged to go polish up their résumés.

Some slick old defense attorneys (called "catfishes" in our grimy hallway parlance) would try to game the system by instructing clients who were free on bail to remain outside the courtroom until the cops who were there to testify against them gave up waiting and left court for the day. The lawyers prevent the relevant case from being called by staying busy with other matters or by leaving the room to take care of business in other courtrooms. Once the officers who were going to testify are gone, the defense would answer "ready" for whatever hearing, meaning that the prosecution would need a Motion State continuance to get their officer witnesses back to court. If that can be done a few times in a row, or maybe even just once if the timing is right, it "runs the term" and the defense can get a default "gotcha" win they don't deserve.

The simple fact is that many clients who are out on bail arrive late to court. It's not good enough to arrive at any time before the call ends; a specific requirement of bail is to be present at the time the call is scheduled to begin. Technically, just being late can count as failing to appear, and failing to appear in court results in the issuance of an arrest warrant. Some judges tolerate late arrivals and allow lawyers to "pass the case" to wait for their clients to appear, rather than go through the hassle of issuing warrants that will need to be either recalled or enforced just a few minutes later. Other judges just issue bond forfeiture warrants (BFWs) immediately if the defendant isn't in the courtroom when his or her case gets called by the clerk. Lawyers who know that their clients are late can go to the clerk and request not to call the case until the lawyer indicates he or she is ready. If that's not possible, the attorney needs to pay attention like a hawk for the moment the case is called and then shout out an instant request to pass the matter, with the hope that the docket is busy enough that the judge's priority is to just move forward with whatever is ready instead of pausing to ask why a matter that's just been called needs to be passed.

In one of my earliest career appearances before that veteran judge, I had a client who was late to court, so I was trying to stall in order to prevent a situation where he'd get hooked on a BFW that had been issued just minutes before his arrival. By the time he did show up, the cops who were there to testify against him had been released by the courtroom ASAs. Releasing officers is a very common professional courtesy if the officers have come to court directly after finishing a night shift and the matter for which they've appeared is not going to proceed. Not knowing about the unspoken protocols of eating an unwanted continuance as the price for avoiding a BFW, I answered ready for the hearing simply because my client finally arrived and I was ready.

The judge was irate and started screaming at me about this shady tactic of "gaming the term," basically threatening me to retract my "ready for hearing" answer and take the continuance Motion Defendant, or he would hold me in contempt or otherwise make my life miserable in his courtroom going forward. I had no idea what he was talking about, and so I frantically passed the case and ran to get my supervisor. My boss had to go to the judge's chambers and convince him that I was clueless about the scam, and then he stood up and took the continuance for me, just so that I didn't have to go back in there and risk any further ire.

Eventually, I won a major jury trial and a series of bench trials before that judge, during the course of which he came to his own more deeply informed conclusions about the authenticity of my representations and my efforts to defend my clients. Nothing commands respect like winning, and it completely changed the trajectory of our relationship to the point that not only was I assigned to his calls whenever possible, but I would also use any and all substitution tricks that were available in order to redirect cases away from other judges and get them in front of him. Turned out that he'd ascended to the bench after many years as an assistant attorney general who'd been assigned to prosecute tax cases that were investigated by the father of one of my best buddies from law school. Having overcome extremely rocky beginnings and discovered our connection of mutual friends, I was very lucky to count the Honorable Gerald T. Rohrer among my early mentors in the system.

All of which explains how I drew a regular assignment to work Judge Rohrer's violation of probation (VOP) calls. VOPs are a particular problem for defense attorneys; not that the original charges are that bad—obviously to get probation in the first place instead of being sent to jail or prison, chances are that the underlying crime was nonviolent and the defendant didn't have a long rap sheet. The reason it's terrible for the defense is because the process is nothing like a trial: the defendant has very limited procedural rights, there are far fewer defenses to argue, the punishment options are worse, and the defendant has already gotten his or her break and allegedly blown it. More often than not, the whole thing comes down to begging for mercy to avoid a custodial sentence by trying to make promises on behalf of people you don't really know that they can be trusted to avoid repeating the same exact mistakes they've already made. It's a losing game, and the defendant's best play is to rely on the rapport between attorney and judge.

Probationers who were PD clients at sentencing do not automatically remain PD clients throughout their terms of probation, but public defenders get reappointed at VOP hearings if the defendant is in jail or if the violation is serious enough that the defendant is likely to be arrested in court, known as "getting swept" or being "taken off the floor." When a VOP case gets called before the judge for its first hearing, some judges will appoint a PD immediately and pass the case to let the lawyer get familiar with the details and try to intervene in a constructive way. Other judges enjoy toying with their prey and will make the defendant stand and speak alone for a bit to let them dig their hole a little deeper. Until the judge says the magic words "PD appointed," there is nothing we can do except sit there and watch them squirm.

During those times when we are sitting there waiting to be appointed, we usually make an effort to build professional relationships with the other courtroom staff. In addition to the judges who run the show, there are clerks, court reporters, deputies, Pretrial Services or Probation Department staff, and of course prosecutors. As much as some people might underestimate or dismiss the quality of legal representation that's provided by the Public Defender's Office, there is no substitute for the direct relationships we develop and the opportunities for advocacy that derive from them. There is a high rate of failure to be sure, but especially in plea discussions, PDs can use our dedication and interpersonal credibility to win our clients bits of freedom that would otherwise be taken away.

The deputy who was regularly assigned as courtroom security

for Judge Rohrer's VOP calls was a giant of a guy who'd grown up in Evanston, next to where I grew up in Skokie. We were only a few years apart in age; he was an army veteran and the son of a cop, and I was the son of a veteran and a lawyer. We both liked sports and had plenty of time to shoot the breeze during slow call afternoons. He loved to mess with me during low-intensity moments to try to derail my train of thought. One time when I was in front of the bench discussing continuance dates with the judge, a very attractive woman walked into the courtroom and caught everyone's momentary attention. The deputy leaned in close to my ear and whispered in a mock-hillbilly accent, "I'd pick the corn from her shit." I had to pretend I was having a coughing fit in order to take a pause and regain my composure.

The absolute essence of being a defense attorney was expressed to me by my first boss as "Get them out, and keep them out." Given that the point of probation is conditional freedom, most of the defendants in VOP calls walk into the courtroom off the street. Those of us who defend them would like to see them leave through the same door they came in, but inevitably some get swept, and we find ourselves facing them in a holding cell as the deputy catalogs their shoelaces and personal items, while we collect phone numbers to help with arranging things like picking up their kids and making bail. The routine always starts the same; handcuffs generally aren't used in the courtroom so as not to violate the sanctity of our chapel of American freedom. Someone being taken into custody is immediately sandwiched by two courtroom deputies, who tell the detainee to place his hands behind his back and walk to the lockup door. Once inside, the search process begins. Some sheriffs let us PDs work while this is going on, but some make us wait until that part is over. Especially with VOPs, the sheriffs want a quick moment to go ask the judge if their intent is to keep the defendant in or just give a "time-out," because other parts of processing such as fingerprinting and photographing will be skipped if the point is just to shock the defendant awake with a catch and release.

Toward the end of an otherwise quiet VOP afternoon, a guy walked in who had exhausted all the standard excuses for his fumbling noncompliance and was taken off the floor. The deputy left me with him for a minute while he went to check on the judge's intentions. This guy was staying, so he had to be processed for transport to actual jail. The deputy told him, "Take everything out of your pockets," so he reached in and pulled a few things out like keys and a bus ticket, some crumpled receipts, that sort of stuff. As soon as that was over, the deputy put the detainee on the wall in the frisk position. Cops will almost always ask the people they're about to frisk if there is anything in their clothing that will cut or prick them: the question serves the dual purpose of protecting officer safety and producing easy off-guard confessions. I was sitting two feet away copying information from the court file to my own, so I wasn't really looking at first, but I heard everything. Getting a denial of anything sharp or dangerous, the search proceeded.

The detainee wasn't up there for more than a few seconds when the deputy felt more stuff in his pockets. The sheriff was the kind of officer who was willing to give people the benefit of the doubt, but still reiterated his instructions with a sense of frustration: "I said *everything*."

"Sorry, here." He reached into his pockets and grabbed more junk, except this time there were some coins mixed in too. Coins make deputies concerned; they are hard to miss if you're trying to empty your pockets, and they can be thrown—hard—if you're looking to cause trouble. Metal projectiles in a jail are not what security is all about.

Before he went to search the detainee some more, the deputy pressed him against the wall with one arm and asked very directly, "Are you *sure* that's all?"

"Yeah, I'm sure."

Now I was paying attention to their interaction because the stakes were that much higher. My friend the deputy turned my new client around and put him back on the wall. Sure enough, with the kind of careful examination one might expect of the circumstances, within a short amount of time he comes up with a lighter the guy had stashed somewhere in his crotch. It turned out that he had a suspicion he would end up being taken in and wanted to have this thing with him to improve his situation in the jail. I had rarely seen that sheriff even slightly mad before, and he maintained his authoritative composure while he said it, but the deputy growled in an unmistakable tone: "I gave you two chances. Now we have to do this the hard way."

There was nothing I could say or do except back off and watch as the deputy cuffed him and headed for the elevator that separated the courtroom holding cells from the basement pens. The elevators were made of lowest-bidder-thin metal, surrounded by a cinder-block shaft. Any noise from them tended to echo, especially bulky officers, rowdy prisoners, and their respective jingling metal tool belts and bracelets. After they got in and the doors closed, I could very clearly hear a series of banging noises that sounded a lot like a body being slammed from side to side, but might've just been the noise of a thorough search taking place in a confined space. Then it quieted down for a minute or two, the doors opened up again, and the two of them came out with very different demeanors.

When they returned to the interview room, nobody told me what happened, and at that moment, I didn't ask. But I must have had a certain look on my face that was enough to register my concern with the sheriff and caused him to feel obligated to explain. He proffered one of the most succinct expressions of raw practicality that I've ever heard and that I'll never forget. It explained what I'd seen in Holiday Bond Court years before, it guided my expectations for every jail visit I ever conducted from then on, and it taught me the absolute essence of the cop mentality.

As straight-faced as a man could be, the deputy just said: "Either *we're* in charge, or *they* are."

II. INVESTIGATIONS

Every criminal case is based on an accusation of conduct. Trial proceedings are a contest of proof about that alleged conduct, intentionally structured as an adversarial competition between two opponents. Law students are taught that the adversarial system represents the distilled wisdom of centuries of literal trial-and-error in the inherently complex and imperfect process of the administration of justice on the basis of facts that are not always knowable, while balancing the public need for effective security against prevention of arbitrary authoritarian abuses. While it's true that the prosecution always has the obligation to produce sufficient evidence to prove the defendant's guilt beyond a reasonable doubt, the format of litigation as a contest between the parties inevitably changes the essence of the trial process from a pure exercise in truth into a sort of artificial game where neither party has to be fundamentally correct in order to win—they just have to beat the other side. Once that game theory framework set in for me, my logical inference was that if the defense takes the correct strategic approach, then theoretically it should be possible to win every time.

Except theory is far from practice.

Cases are primarily about the truth, even allowing for the different purposes that each side seeks it. The main mission of law-enforcement agencies is to determine what happened, find the person or persons responsible, and punish them as a means to preserve order. The main mission of the defense is to prevent injustices by identifying flaws in the prosecution's case, either in the ultimate proof it provides or in the process by which it was built. These are entirely distinct exercises, but they share a common core of gaining significant adversarial advantage by being correct about the facts. That's why the significance of the case investigation cannot be overstated in criminal law. A blizzard of other factors come into play in determining the final outcome of a given case, an important one of which is pure luck, but a strong investigation gives the lawyers great confidence that they are inarguably correct about the crucial details of timelines, locations, events, perspectives, and individuals. The details are essential in forming a cohesive strategy around all the seals and gaps of proof, and stains or strengths of character, for the exhibits, assertions, and witnesses that may be produced at trial.

Prosecutors win an overwhelming percentage of criminal trials due to the combination of unambiguous political favoritism and incomparable investigative advantage. There is no defense substitute for the political, financial, scientific, and personnel resources that the government can marshal for prosecutors. Their investigators are the FBI, massive forces like the Chicago Police Department, or networks of multiple professional law-enforcement agencies from the feds right down to the local sheriff. Calls to 911 can, and usually do, prompt immediate action to arrive on scene and bear firsthand witness to critical events or to interview people with fresh and vivid recollections of them. At the scene of the crime, investigators collect fresh physical evidence and contextual information, and can leverage the power of jail to persuade or dissuade cooperation as needed. Taken together, that is a formula for investigative domination. First responders' evidentiary collection and analysis is then subject to the prosecution's absolute power and discretion to decide whether to bring a case or not and, if so, on what specific grounds. Simply put, if the prosecution is doing its job professionally and ethically, they should never lose.

Defense investigations are a world apart. We are always working from behind, literally, since defense investigations are framed within the terms set out by the police and prosecution, and are usually conducted long after the events at issue have occurred. For public defenders in particular, since our clients are overwhelmingly incarcerated, systemic delay compounds the disadvantages of secondary investigations. In Cook County, specific steps of pretrial procedure are usually handled at different courthouses on separate dates, with continuances of a week or more between each step. These typically include bond hearings to establish probable cause to detain the arrestee and set a bail amount, and in felony cases, a separate preliminary hearing to establish probable cause for the particular charges. Preliminary hearings can happen before a judge or a grand jury, but they both involve witness testimony, usually by police officers who are assigned specific "key" dates for court hearings when they are not on patrol. Despite these key dates, there are various reasons why officers may not be able to appear in court, and they are afforded wide professional courtesy in rescheduling by continuances. A finding of probable cause is then followed by an appearance before the chief judge for each case to be sent to a specific trial court, with those assignments based on a combination of factors, including the location of the arresting police district, the severity of the offense, and the weight of judicial caseload. Only after all of that does the case appear for the first time in its trial court, where the defendant is presented with the formal charges and has a public defender officially appointed on their behalf if they cannot afford their own counsel. At this point, the PD enters a plea and begins the discovery process.

This kind of timeline means that it's typically more than a month after an arrest before the first meeting occurs between the client and the assistant public defender who will be handling the case. In

Chicago and its surrounding suburbs, the practical effect is that the defendant has been in the Cook County Jail for an extended stretch already before they even meet their lawyer. The sprawling jail is rife with gang pressures, outright sadistic violence, punitive procedures and enforcement, retrenched health care, sordid food, constant noise and stench, systemic sleep deprivation under the constant glare of fluorescent lights, and all the other attendant features of inner-urban incarceration.

This is why the bond system is a form of blackmail.

Believe me, most people who serve time in the Cook County Jail are ready to do whatever it takes to get out, even if "getting out" means moving on to prison. They will take pleas; readily forgo investigations and possible defenses; agree to impossibly draconian probationary conditions; waive procedural, trial, and appeal rights; and even acquiesce to prison sentences—just to "get out of county." Many times I was in the midst of introductory conversations when my client just demanded: "Go get me an offer."

For the cases that do proceed to exploring possible defenses, it's that first meeting between attorney and client where the investigation begins in earnest. Courthouses have behind-the-scenes lockups that are discreetly networked throughout the building and kept relatively clean so that they are both secure and palatable to the judges who are forced, however briefly, to confront the reality of human beings in cages. Courthouse lockups have a routine, and that routine includes familiar sounds. The morning arrival of the prisoners is noisy with movement, voices, radio chatter, heavy motorized locking doors, and the jingling of keys and restraint chains. A deputy sheriff brings a list of prisoners out of the lockup, and the courtroom public defenders are expected to cross-reference that list with the cases on the court call. That way the PDs know who is there for their first appearance in the trial court, called an arraignment, and can then go into the lockup and ask that person if they've already hired a private attorney, if they need more time to do so, or if they can't afford one. Incarcerated people who cannot afford private counsel become our clients. We get the charges from the court file and ask the sheriff to bring that person to the interview room, a feature of every courthouse lockup that is required to respect the defendant's right to counsel and a fundamental pillar of that right, the attorney-client privilege. The choiceless coupling of court-appointed lawyer and client is about to begin, and there is much to gain or lose in first impressions.

Meeting a new client involves an interpersonal dynamic that each PD has to grasp in dealing with the breadth of humanity and the trauma each person is going through. Sometimes the interaction is oddly rote and perfunctory, like when the defendant is a frequent flier who wants to plead out a simple case. There is a vast underclass of people who seem accustomed to being arrested, and both they and many courthouse apparatchiks become numb to the revolving door and inevitability of being in the system. Allegations of racism and classism gain a lot of traction there, just seeing who comes through the door and the mechanized way they are processed and packaged for what the staff call "disposal."

Other times there are people who have never been arrested before, or who have no idea what they're being charged with (despite having been in jail for a month or more already), or have been charged with extremely serious offenses. They can be scared, ashamed, angry, hurt, sick . . . in just about any mental or physical distress you can imagine. They are still entering into the worst experience of their lives—maybe the defining experience of their lives—and their PD might be the first somewhat friendly person they can talk to and ask for help. But even as their PD, they don't know you personally and didn't choose you to be their lawyer; to them, PDs in general (and you in particular) represent "the system" that has taken them into custody against their will. We have to try to establish some trust by being part psychologist, part medic, part cleric, and, of course, all parts lawyer to provide the communication, explanation, compassion, and representation they desperately need. An innate ability to empathize and a professional ability to balance these interests are huge reasons why a person becomes a public defender in the first place.

Even if an individual PD isn't the lead attorney for a particular defendant and therefore has no control over the full investigation or strategy that will be used at trial, we have those moments to record professional impressions and details that might be crucial. We are seeing the defendant's physical condition and wardrobe at a specific moment in time. I recall at least one instance where notes of an APD saying that the defendant was missing one shoe at the time of their initial meeting served as a critical point of proof to exonerate him down the line. PDs and our investigators are routinely required to document physical injuries that occur post arrest, which may be important in motions to exclude evidence or in lawsuits for damages. We are hearing the defendant's immediate reaction to the charges and reports, and given what's in them, we ask for their immediate suggestions in building a defense. As a matter of priority, we ask them for witnesses to the alleged events or the arrest. Details of their arrest need to be confirmed because procedure is critical to the defense, and every investigation has to be centered on the scene of the alleged event. Because of ethical duties against presenting testimony we know to be false, and because of the strategic need to keep open as many options as possible, PDs never ask a defendant point-blank: "Did you do it?" We explain the legal process, review with the defendant any evidence that is available so far (which is usually an incomplete set of police reports), and discuss possible investigative measures that can be taken to build a defense.

To put the investigation into motion, PDs don't get the limitless resources and an international array of specialist agencies like the prosecution does. In the Public Defender's Office, most of us are assigned to work with a single investigator whose time is shared with several other attorneys. Our investigators take no initiative and make no strategic suggestions; the investigative actions to be taken are the exclusive responsibility of the attorneys. With limited exceptions, the investigators are there to serve our subpoenas, accompany us on scene visits to take photos and measurements, and act as "provers" for our interviews. To the best of my knowledge and belief, they get no substantive law-enforcement training of any kind since they are not first responders and are not expected to confront danger. In fact, in the event of danger, they are tasked with helping the attorney get out of there as fast as possible, but are not necessarily required to see that imperative through. For the most part, I have no idea how PD investigators find their profession, since it's not the sort of thing someone grows up dreaming to become. Nevertheless, their work is crucial and in high demand. Having a good investigator was a perk that was reserved by the supervisors for the attorneys who needed them the most. You can tell a lot about a lawyer by the assignments they give their investigators, and whether those assignments are frequent and creative, or rote and routine as part of what we called the "CYA" (cover your ass) school of thought.

My right-hand man was a guy from the Far South Side of the city who had extensive experience on both sides of the law. Unfortunately, he did not actually have a complete right hand. Ralph lost all four fingers—but not his thumb—in an industrial accident in the 1970s when he worked at the *Sun-Times* newspaper printing plant on the Near Northwest Side, just outside the Loop. Surgeries that initially sewed his hand to his stomach to regenerate his skin had finally left him with a stump of doughy folds pulled over and sealed shut. The irregular hairs and patchy circulation gave the whole thing a look and feel somewhat like a large, dry, gelatinous turkey drumstick with a single opposable digit. He took great joy in thrusting that thing out at introductions, offering what he could as his form of handshake. He was totally unabashed when it came to extending, discussing, examining, waving around, and generally focusing on that hand. Extremely comfortable with it himself, he was testing everyone's fortitude, which he loved doing. He was far more interested in, rather than afraid of, the reaction of strangers because it let him get a very quick read on the type of person with whom he was dealing. I recognized his angle from the beginning and absolutely reveled in teasing him—not to mock his disability, but the show he made of it, and to build our bond.

For a very high portion of PD investigations, it's absolutely critical to just *go check*. Check the details of the narrative that the police have laid out, and check what the defendant tells you. Go to the scene and observe the physical layout to view sight lines, lighting, cameras, distances, and see what else is there that isn't in the reports. Ideally, the PD and investigator go around the same time of day as the incident, on the same day of the week, during the same season of the year, in order to recreate as closely as possible the circumstances that existed at the relevant time.

Then we interview witnesses, which can be difficult because most people refuse to say anything that could lead them to being required to testify against someone they fear. In some investigations, potential witnesses might be afraid of the person who's been arrested; but in many defense investigations, potential witnesses are usually afraid of the police. The defense can't be out there to protect a witness if anyone comes for direct or indirect revenge, which has happened in the past. Cops are particularly savvy about leveraging their power to protect themselves. Knowing that witnesses can have particular motivations to talk or remain silent, we have to make a judgment call about their reliability. Unfortunately, this has to include asking if they have a criminal background, which immediately drives a wedge between us and them. Every single prosecutor in the world will get this information reliably, and they are prepared to use that—sometimes only that—as an entire cross-examination if necessary. Since so many judges are former prosecutors, it's not wrong to say that virtually any prior conviction can completely ruin your witness, no matter what they have to say. Very often we find ourselves going into high-crime neighborhoods or housing projects and trying to find credible witnesses who don't have any "background" and are willing and able to take time off work (or whatever else they do all day) in order to travel all the way across the city or county to testify against the police, all without any compensation or personal benefit, only to return home and face whatever possible harassment or repercussions may come without the benefit of any protection from the ones who exposed them to that risk.

The chances of success are, let's just say, not very darn good.

That's why usually the best defense evidence is the pictures, the measurements, the timeline, and the contradictions or material omissions in the police reports. People might be surprised to find out just how often the defense finds some evidence to suggest that the police "clean up" their cases with fixes such as exaggerations, simplifications, convenient omissions, streamlining, and outright lies, however large or small. There aren't any scientific studies I'm aware of concerning the frequency and impact of police lies because that would require cops to admit to, or be convicted of, criminal acts of perjury and violations of civil rights in order to have reliable data. Quite simply, the government does not want to know the answer. Nobody can prove exactly how often cops lie, or precisely measure the significance of a particular untruth. But every defense attorney can give you anecdotes and examples of lies they've uncovered, sometimes extremely easily, as if the police don't really expect that someone would just go out and check.

By virtue of my courtroom assignment, my cases came from specific districts of the city and included one of Chicago's most notorious public housing project developments, Cabrini-Green. I had to schedule days out of court to do my investigations in the morning because Ralph flatly refused to go into the projects after eleven a.m. His theory, or at least the one he subscribed to, was that junkies and gangbangers had a distinct general behavioral pattern of waking up late and getting to their first fixes and sales of the day in the late morning. If we waited until noon, it was too late to accomplish anything constructive, and too dangerous as well.

There were several risks for us in the projects. Cabrini-Green in particular was a cluster of mostly high-rise buildings where the sidewalks that approached each tower were easily visible from gated external hallways and stairwells that made perfect spotters' nests. Even approaching them had a ritual because there were gang look-outs on the upper floors at all hours, and our profile resembled police enough to merit the standard rooftop hollers that served as sentry reports. We knew that someone was always watching us walk and might be considering whether it was worth it or not to take a shot. We found ourselves well aware of the attention we drew, and our possible paths of escape and cover, but going early in the morning helped to tamp down the fear of death to just a morbid background concern.

Then there was the issue of getting upstairs. The elevators almost never worked anyway, and there was no escape if we got cornered in there, so we always took the stairs. The stairwells reeked of urine and dumpster juice—that liquefied rotted trash that collects over months at a time. The lighting was usually broken on purpose by the gang spotters. We had to listen for any types of gatherings that we didn't want to stumble across and witness unintentionally. After all, for a combination of reasons that included being excluded from the legal definition of law-enforcement officers and concerns about potential liability, we were required to be unarmed.

Ralph was first teaching me how to navigate the Cabrini-Green stairwells in 1997, the year Girl X was attacked. A nine-year-old girl was using the stairs to go from her friend's apartment, where she'd been at a sleepover, back up to her grandmother's unit, so that she could change her clothes and get her backpack before heading to school. She was grabbed in the stairwell by a predator who took her back to his apartment and repeatedly raped her in seemingly every possible way. During the attack she soiled herself, which I would later learn is common for rape victims. The perpetrator was apparently disgusted by the mess and became more aggressive as a result, which I also learned is common for sex attackers. The perpetrator choked the girl nearly to death, and as she lay there totally defenseless, she was stabbed, defiled with gang symbols written on her body, poisoned with pesticide sprayed down her throat, and left in the stairwell to die. She survived but suffered profound injuries that put her in a coma and caused permanent disabilities that included being rendered almost entirely mute and blind.

The poor victim was so young and vulnerable, yet had been so unspeakably brutalized that even in a city like Chicago, and even in a place like Cabrini-Green, there was a spasm of wild outrage. An anxious but initially fruitless manhunt only made it worse. Journalistic ethics required that the victim not be publicly named due to her age, so the press dubbed her "Girl X." With the media attention and pressure building steadily, the cops turned those buildings inside-out looking for suspects. They had no shortage of resources: there was a police station located directly across the street, an entire semi-separate force of Chicago Housing Authority Police in and around the buildings 24/7, constant patrols, databases of residents and known offenders, and an army of plainclothes officers assigned to proactive squads called tactical units who conduct street stops and searches every single day of the year. But even with all of that as standard operating procedure for Cabrini-Green, the tension in those buildings hit new heights for Girl X.

It's not like I didn't know that things like that were possible or had occurred. I don't think I was particularly naive about the existence of child predators, or sex crimes, or people whose hearts are so cold that they can harm, rape, or kill and then go about their day like nothing happened. I wasn't connected to that girl personally and was still years away from having a daughter of my own, which of course changed the way I related to the suffering of parents whose children were victims of crimes. But that was the first time I felt a personal connection to a headline atrocity, and it was just because I was there, in those buildings, in those stairwells, probably on the very landing where that poor child's life changed forever. Everybody knew that Cabrini-Green was dangerous to the point of almost existing in a different realm, like a parallel universe that was technically in the city but definitely a world apart. They teach you lots of things in law school, and then additional layers of information are added during internships and formative experiences at the elbow of senior mentors. You think you are prepared to be an objective professional, right up until the moment you're standing in the spot where evil happened, smelling it, hearing it, sensing it, and wondering how on earth people can hurt anyone like that, let alone little girls.

About three weeks after that attack, Ralph and I needed to visit the scene of an arrest for a client in the same building. It concerned a drug case of a somewhat serious variety—possession of a controlled substance with intent to deliver, or "PCS w/I" for short—that involved a substantial amount of cocaine. The defendant was looking at serious time, and since he was accused of dealing out of a Chicago Housing Authority (CHA) apartment, his family faced being evicted too. As a way around the general constitutional requirement that police get warrants to search houses, the cops were claiming that they were simply walking down the hallway when they looked in the window of our client's apartment and were able to see him weighing and packaging cocaine in plain view. They also claimed that he was doing that with his apartment door open, so they didn't need to force entry. Many cases come down to police testimony against the word of, well, criminals, and no matter how ridiculous a scenario might seem, there are plenty of judges who look for any basis to support the police and will find their version more credible than virtually any defendant's denial.

At that time PDs weren't even given work computers, let alone expensive investigative tools like cars. Ralph and I drove to our investigations in his Toyota, which had custom plates denoting the year that he got sober. There were parking lots near the main high-rise buildings of Cabrini, set back from Division Street and the surrounding streets by driveways that could be several hundred feet long, depending on the direction of approach. On our drive into the lot, we were passed by one of the ubiquitous CPD tactical units. From the very beginning of my street work, whenever we passed officers near a scene we were working, I would look to see if they were the cops involved in my case, in order to take mental notes about how they looked and behaved away from court.

That day the two-man crew hawked us back, fixated on us in what I initially perceived as standard part of scanning the area for suspicious activity, except they held their stare too long. Ralph got nervous immediately, but I was quite confident that our authoritative mission put us beyond reproach. However, as soon as our cars passed each other, they cut a U-turn to our back bumper, and I could see their strobing turn signals and headlights that signaled we were about to have a conversation. I forget the exact expletives that Ralph was muttering, but he was not happy that I had invited confrontation by staring them down. As he chose a safe spot to pull over, he was telling me not to make any sudden moves, and I remember thinking he was being too dramatic.

I could see in the side mirror that they both got out to approach our car. I could also see that the officer on my side had unsnapped the strap of his holster and had his hand on his gun, although he hadn't drawn it out. It was still two years before the separate police shootings on the same summer night in 1999, one of an unarmed driver, Robert Russ, and the other of an unarmed passenger, LaTanya Haggerty, that widely exposed the real dangers of not showing your hands (or having anything in them) during a traffic stop in Chicago, but I had read many reports of these interactions going very badly very quickly. That was the first time I was really on the business end of a CPD tactical stop, so I put my hands in front of me on the dash with my fingers spread out wide to let the officer get a good view of how empty they were as he advanced from our rear bumper toward my window.

The officer who approached Ralph's side bent forward from his position of cover aligned with the B pillar, took a look at the two of us, and got straight to the point: "What're two white guys doin' at Cabrini-Green?" They hadn't recognized us from court or by our profile, and they hadn't seen us commit any traffic violation or any other illegal act. Theirs was a simple, race-based bias that we couldn't possibly be there for any legal purpose. When we told them we were from the PD's Office and showed them our credentials, they instantly seemed to realize that they were committing civil rights violations against two county employees on the job, including an attorney. They satisfied themselves that our county IDs were solid and walked back to their car about as quickly as they could. But before they drove away, they pulled up next to Ralph and asked as a sort of *mea culpa* if we wanted their help to locate anyone or get access to someplace inside the buildings. We demurred with a professional "No thanks, guys." Setting aside considerations of attorney-client privilege over the things we might find, we didn't want to be seen with them. We had enough problems getting people to talk to us once we explained that we were trying to collect potential evidence against the cops. We didn't need the added problem of folks thinking we were the cops before we even got there.

Our client went by his street nickname "Deuce." He was insisting that he was not packaging cocaine so brazenly in the open; that not only had he covered his windows with taped-up sheets and garbage bags, but he had actually closed and locked his door, more like you might expect from someone engaged in highly illegal and obviously dangerous activities in Cabrini-Green. We went to the CHA management offices where they had records of giving Deuce citations for repeatedly covering up his windows with various tarps, even though there were rules against that. We also talked to the maintenance man who had been assigned to repair Deuce's kicked-in door on the day of his arrest. The maintenance crew had taken pictures to show that the work was completed as assigned, and the damage to the door-jamb and the window coverings were clearly visible in the photos.

Deuce wasn't denying that he was packaging cocaine at his kitchen table, but we proved that the search and arrest were done in violation of the Constitution, and the cops were lying about key details, and so the evidence collected during the arrest could not be used at trial and the charges had to be dropped.

Not long after Ralph and I had our tactical encounter, the police made an arrest in the Girl X case too. After working through an exceptionally long list of potential suspects, they focused on a repeat offender with a prior sex offense who was initially implicated just by being near the scene at the time the crime occurred. They didn't have any physical evidence to use—in fact, they destroyed what little there was before the defense could test it or it could be preserved for future analysis—but they said the suspect made several statements that amounted to confessions. He was an epileptic with low intellect whom they questioned over the course of several days while they withheld his anti-seizure medication, but he had allegedly told them where to find the can of roach spray that was used in the attack, and they claimed to find it right where he said it would be. The State got their conviction, and the defendant got 120 years. Maybe they got the right guy, but the interrogation tactics and the destruction of the physical evidence struck me as classic indications of a cover-up. And that number shocked me too. It's not possible to regard someone as having any human value while imposing a 120-year prison sentence on them. When I express my opinions about such punishments to people who support that kind of retribution, their embrace of the inherent message of such sentences makes me genuinely afraid of the sadistic punishment fetish that runs through certain strains of American society.

Ralph and I went to Cabrini-Green many times, for many cases. We talked about that little girl almost every time we went into those buildings, and we kept the dangers of the stairwells at the forefront of our minds.

III. REDEMPTION

Ralph grew up in the South Shore neighborhood of the city close to Jackson Park, near 79th and Stony Island. That area is one of many places where Chicago consists of rows and rows of bungalows, color-dyed brick and aluminum siding, small square lawns and carriage walks, dotted by trees that were planted as saplings at about the same time each new foundation was laid. Ralph recalled South Shore as a white working-class neighborhood around the time he was born in 1954 that started to transition in the '60s into the black community it is today. His father, Charlie, moved the family once in response to the changes, but only a few blocks away, since they wanted to stay close to Charlie's mother. In fact, they bought the place right next door to hers.

Ralph described his dad as being as blue-collar as they come, working as a washing-machine repairman for Sears when he started his family. Grandma worked as a receptionist for General Felt Industries (GFI), which was built into one of the largest carpet-padding companies in the world by Theodore Horwich, a prominent Jewish philanthropist as well as businessman. After a few years, Ralph was the oldest of four, and Grandma was able to use her connections to get Charlie a job with Cortland Cartage Co., the trucking company that delivered GFI's padding. That turned out to be the starting point of Ralph's education in Chicago crime.

The truck drivers were union guys with the Teamsters. Local historians and federal indictments paint a picture of seventy years of gangster control of the Teamsters by contemporaries and heirs of Al Capone—men like Cornelius Shea and "Big Tim" Murphy in Chicago, and nationally by the likes of Jimmy Hoffa. Some of the tactics they used included manipulating delivery schedules and labor stoppages for bribes, but some were much more simple and direct, like stealing off the trucks.

When Charlie became affiliated, he was given two things: a note to keep in his pocket with a particular phone number to use in case of emergency, and a special tool to break the band seal on his truck. Tampering with the band seal was a federal offense, but as a low-level Teamster he did what he was told, and what he was told to do was to "knock down the count" on his deliveries. At each stop on his route, he'd use various distraction techniques or just plain lies in order to keep maybe five or seven rolls on the truck that were to be sold off-route. He called it "the hustle," and once Ralph was old enough, he was brought along to distract dock workers and then sent to collect the money for the special deliveries. Some of that was kicked back to the boss of the crew, but enough was kept that eventually the family was able to get a nice new car and finally move out of South Shore to a bigger house in the Southwest suburb of Hometown. Dinner conversations would center around "proper" stealing techniques such as how to steal, from whom it was permitted to steal, and the advantages of certain types of protection.

Ralph recalled additional important lessons about how to deal with the law. The same way many people are caught—by some stupid accident—Charlie eventually got caught in a place he was not supposed to be. He had parked his truck to make an unsanctioned delivery and the air bled off the brakes, causing it to roll into a crash. The Teamsters protected their workers with a mix of coercion and physical violence, so no matter how frustrated managers or employers might get, there was no real option to fire them. That was true for Charlie too, even for crashing the truck off-route. But his supervisor, Horwich's brother-in-law Jack Freeman, was angry enough about the pattern of behavior with the drivers that he called in the FBI. Piqued by any chance to make inroads against the Chicago outfit, they sent a couple of agents to conduct interviews.

Ralph shared this story with me a few times over the years; either he forgot that he already told it to me, or it just resonated in new ways. He always recounted it with a certain energetic thrill, as though he had been there himself. There was pride in the narration, both personal and projected, because there was an element of legal strategy that elevated the lesson above a truck-driving Teamster in trouble with the law and gave it a lasting quality along the lines of a similar theme that we were constantly trying to impart on our clients in the streets.

The agents were in Freeman's office, an older man and a younger one. Freeman was there too, looking smug and aggressive, making comments about how they "had 'im this time." The agents laid out a narrative of facts and conclusions that painted a fairly complete picture of understanding how schemes worked, who reported to whom, missing padding rolls, unauthorized route stops, connections, profits made and missing, and Teamster control. Charlie had the phone number in his pocket, but was damn sure he didn't need it. He listened. He smoked. He kept completely cool, waiting for them to make their demands that were certain to include a plea for him to roll over on someone, followed by some false promise of help if he just cooperated. It was all he could do to suppress a laugh.

Finally, he asked with a daring tone: "Am I under arrest?" No direct answer, just more twisted cajoling. Again: "Am I under arrest?" Freeman was fuming, watching it play out quite differently than he'd imagined. The agents had given their best pitch and squeeze, and Charlie was having none of it. Receiving no answer, he simply said, "No? Then I'm leaving." And with that, he got up and walked out. He must've been beaming from ear to ear when he told friends and family the tale of coming face-to-face with the FBI and not having flinched as he skated through the door. The lesson, as always: Keep your mouth shut. Never admit to anything. "Dummy up" and, if you can, walk. Ralph learned these lines as mantras, the crux of life lessons from a father to his firstborn: "Dummy up" and "Spot the hustle."

These lessons were mixed with a steady stream of what Ralph called "basic '60s bigotry of South Shore people," but he said his grandma balanced that out. She was adamant that the Jews in general, and the Horwiches in particular, were good people. On the few occasions Ralph tried to copy his father's bigoted words or deeds in front of his grandmother or mother, he'd get a smack and a lecture: "Just because your father gets away with that, don't think you can. They're people no different from you."

Ralph talked about his mom being aware of the extra challenge it would be to keep him on the straight and narrow given his paternal influence, and how she wasn't up to it herself. She had learned from her own Catholic upbringing that corporal punishment need not be spared. Ralph forced himself to endure belt or hairbrush beatings without giving his mother either the satisfaction of seeing him suffer, or the benefit of believing he was learning anything. His mom had made a rare concession to Charlie in leaving the Catholic Church to become a Lutheran, but at least a piece of her heart remained with the archdiocese. That part was reawakened when Ralph was just a kid, when one of the most heart-wrenching events in Chicago history happened in the late 1950s.

On December 1, 1958, in a Catholic elementary school called Our Lady of the Angels, a fire killed ninety-two children and three teachers. Not only did the story dominate international headlines, but a picture of a fireman carrying the limp body of a child he couldn't rescue before smoke inhalation claimed that innocent soul was the cover of *Life* magazine, the premier pictorial chronicle of American existence at the time. Shivers of anguish gripped Chicagoans, at least anyone with empathy, in all corners of the city. It would be tough to imagine a more cruel formula of suffering than one that includes the sanctuary of a school, the shelter of a church, the purity of youth, the holy spirit of Christmas, and the capricious sear of inferno and toxic fumes.

Irish Catholic cops and firemen of the Near West Side saw reflections of themselves and images of their brethren in the corpses they had to cradle and collect from the soot and soaked ashes. No logic-loving intellectual admits to harboring a belief in ghosts, but anytime Ralph and I found ourselves in Humboldt Park, we stood at Iowa and Avers and could almost hear an anguished wailing echo through time. He was only four years old when it happened, and I was almost two decades away from being born, but we were far from alone in feeling connected to the children who perished there. Go stand there and breathe the air that those little kids couldn't claw in with desperate lungs; a tiny hand just might take hold of yours and make a cross, no matter what religion you embrace or reject.

Unfortunately, for the nearly opposite effect, we could simply visit the St. Paul Lutheran School in Oak Lawn where Ralph spent his formative years. From fourth to eighth grades, he was subject to not only the physical discipline that was the hallmark of parochial education, but certain bodily inspections at the hands of a very senior male member of the staff. Much of the attention that's been belatedly heaped on scandals involving the cover-ups of abuse by, and subsequent absolutory reassignments of, predatory priests was focused on the Catholic Church. Far less scrutiny befell the other denominations. Ralph didn't exactly love to talk about it, especially in light of his subsequent renaissance after his addictions and wilder years that he worked so hard to move beyond, but part of dealing with all of it allowed him to share key recollections in his matter-of-fact manner.

His elementary school memories carried the primary association of having been subjected to inspections of his body hair and how he looked in his pants, measurements of his growth, and being questioned about whether or not those inspections by his elders caused secret excitement that could be confided just between them. Grandma was furious, referring to the abuser as "that dirty queer." Ralph recalled not understanding why his grandma was so mad at the time, and clearly remembered a sense of confusion about not being believed by his mother. At least Ralph's church-related trauma was indirectly validated by the subsequent major national scandal that forced a public reckoning and massive awards to victims.

Mine has been conspicuously ignored.

The Catholic Church has a long and complicated history. What some see as salvation, others see as hegemony. There can be no doubt about the goals of crusading evangelism: a religious-based desire for expansionism. Global domination can be defended on the basis of its purported altruistic intentions, but it can also be a quite convenient cover for the much more empirical advantages of power, money, land, and free labor, each of which the Catholic Church has enjoyed to nearly limitless extent.

Some of the church's major social policy initiatives have been targeted toward women and their reproductive behaviors. It's putting it extremely mildly to state that the church has had a lot to say about celibacy, chastity, abortion, marriage, divorce, promiscuity, and prostitution. One of the ways these initiatives manifested themselves was at institutions known as Magdalene Laundries, which were essentially prisons for women whose lifestyle, physical condition, or lack of social status were offensive to sanctimonious local authorities. In particular, those covens of self-righteousness were used to warehouse women who became pregnant out of wedlock. The women could be "rehabilitated" from their sins and put to work, their families could be spared public shame and ostracization, and their babies could be sold, raised in orphanages, or quietly killed by neglect and abuse. As recently as 2014, the remains of 796 babies were discovered in the septic tank of the Bon Secours Mother and Baby Home in Tuam, Ireland.

Magdalene Laundries weren't strictly Catholic, however; there were Protestant ones too. In Ireland, where these facilities had their largest presence, the government gave religious orders enormous power in areas of education and health care, and over ten thousand girls and women were imprisoned in these "asylums for fallen women" throughout that country. The first dedicated Magdalene Laundries were established in the mid-1700s, but by 1800 they had spread to the United States. In the United States, where the relationship between the government and the Catholic Church was fundamentally different than it was in Ireland, the laundries have been described as essentially the first form of women's prisons in America. Most of them were run by a Catholic Order of nuns called the Sisters of the Good Shepherd, but they were absolutely not alone. Perhaps to be expected of any criticism of the church, pushback is intense, and there are scholarly disagreements about the exact nature and length of the activities that occurred in each place. Nevertheless, the essence of these institutions was quite consistent: to facilitate the separation of mothers and their babies. Most scholarly estimates have them disappearing from the United States by the end of the 1970s. The seminal Supreme Court case that protected women's choice to have abortions, *Roe v. Wade*, was decided in 1973 (before being overruled in 2022). Before legal abortion was an option, what happened to 170 years' worth of laundered American babies?

Child trafficking, that's what happened. Polite society lumps most of it under the umbrella of private adoption—which can obviously be legitimate and compassionate—but it also can be the practice of castigating certain women into privatized incarceration, taking their babies away from them, and then selling the babies on a type of black market. Markets need brokers, and America's most prolific baby broker was a woman in Tennessee named Georgia Tann, who operated from Memphis as she orchestrated the seizure and sale of over five thousand babies from 1920 to 1950, right in the center of the American heartland. She's just the most famous—or infamous—

among many such baby brokers who worked with various orders of Catholic and Protestant churches across the country. They found women who were unmarried and pregnant, separated them from their families, took away their babies, and sold them, mostly in the name of ecclesiastical redemption.

Like the complicated history of the church itself, although tremendous good might come from the specific circumstances of a private adoption, each one also guarantees the destruction of the maternal bond, and all the psychological and physiological benefits that derive from it. All I know about my beginnings is that I was born in Tennessee in 1973 to a girl who was sent there from out of state, away from the shame of an out-of-wedlock teenage pregnancy. She ended up giving birth at a private institution that was opened by the Daughters of Charity, a Catholic Order claiming the charism of service to the poor, but who've been found by at least one major governmental inquiry in Scotland to have engaged in systematic physical, sexual, and emotional abuses in their orphanages over the span of many decades.

When my private adoption process was completed, I was flown to Chicago at the age of three days old. Anyone who knew what my adoptive parents went through in order to have children would never question their motives; five full-term stillbirths—including a set of twins, for a total of six dead babies—would probably cause most people enough emotional anguish to become willing to consider every option. After all, desperate times call for desperate measures. I am forever grateful for the good things my parents gave me, but still: Have you ever been hugged by your biological mother? Comforted, consoled, or loved by your biological mother? Have you ever just looked into the eyes of your own biological mother or father? Or even seen pictures of them?

Some of us will never know how any of that feels.

So despite our generational differences, Ralph and I found common ground in our understanding of, and ability to empathize with, personal suffering at the hands of powerful authorities. The similarities were too large to ignore and were often interwoven into our cases. We saw common elements in the backgrounds of many of our clients, sometimes not too different from what we experienced ourselves, whether we were talking about people from South Shore, Cabrini-Green, Skokie, or any of the vast expanse of Cook County in between. As exhilarating as it is to get a "not guilty" verdict or to catch the police in some fundamental transgression against individual rights, being able to touch the humanity of people is the best part of being a public defender. Maybe a little bit selfishly, we both used it as therapy for ourselves.

Ralph was great at it. You need drug treatment? Mental health treatment? A shelter for recovering sex workers? Talk to a guy who knows every aspect of the social service network from deep personal and professional experience and who has connections to every church-run session and outreach pastor from Hometown to Lake Cook Road. He was a drug counselor for the major court-provided rehabilitation service provider TASC (Treatment Alternatives for Safe Communities) before he was an investigator, because he was a junkie before that. We could be working a case involving the Chicago Police MAIU (major accident investigation unit), and he would tell me about his two blackouts behind the wheel, both ending in catastrophic collisions of which he had no memory. He was from the era when cops found drunks like him at the side of the road and would ask what parish he belonged to, and when the answer was satisfactory, they'd tell him to "get a couple hooks in" him and go home rather than making an arrest. He had been a soldier of the army and the mob; exploited, abused, maimed, and ultimately healed through a gauntlet of tribulations of practically biblical proportions, and he came through all of it to find a niche serving the poor and the needy. If anyone understands a person's suffering, or can at least find someone in a specific demographic who certainly does, it's him. We'd be standing in the heart of some gentrified neighborhood like Wicker

Park, cross-referencing arrest addresses with surveillance locations, and he'd break off into a diatribe about Jane Addams's Hull House and the neighborhood history of social services like some kind of dark shadow tour guide with a Jesus streak.

When we left the office to go out into the city and learn about our clients, on the timesheets in the office we wrote "street investigation," but it was so much more than that. There are some demographic probabilities about the people who live in various neighborhoods around Chicago, but there is no substitute for the depth of information you learn about an individual by visiting their home. When you see how they live behind the curtains, you see the things with which they surround themselves, their level of organization or acceptable mess, the pictures and mementos they give pride of place, the smells of their food, their laundry, their furniture, and so on, you get an intimate sense of the tempo and tenor of their daily lives. We talk to them, listen to their stories, and interact with the main characters in their personal narratives of their daily existence. We interview them with a purpose and an authority that creates conditions of revelation. We can ask about anything at all, since they want and need help with a situation that is probably one of the most difficult and dangerous ordeals they've ever experienced. The cops have already physically dominated this person: handcuffed them, transported them to dangerous places, literally stripped and searched their bodies. We come along with the offer of help—assistance not only with the legal aspects, since, let's be honest, there really isn't much we can do in the vast majority of cases—but advocacy that includes a dimension of hopeful rehabilitation. They have problems that maybe nobody has cared about or even acknowledged in any meaningful way up to the moment their PD was appointed. If that PD comes to their home with an investigator to discuss what happened and how to help, they get an interaction with the government of a very different kind than they've ever had before. We can be as much mental health care providers as lawyers and investigators.

Ironically, one of the critical qualifications for being a cop, prosecutor, or judge is that they absolutely must not know from personal experience anything about what it's like to be on the receiving end of the punishments they dish out. Maybe the best chance to educate them comes in the form of private meetings that occur in judges' chambers when the details of plea agreements are hammered out. The trio of judge, prosecutor, and PD who work together on a daily basis can, under the right circumstances of chemistry and good faith, build a sort of bond from the working arrangement that promotes better outcomes than more sterile or confrontational conferences. We have conversations instead of just meetings, and the benefits can be significant.

Building a bond with someone who is literally robed in status far above your own takes time, as well as some confluence of commonality. A stroke of tragedy brought me together with the judge who became the most important influence on my career. The Honorable James R. Epstein had been a highly successful trial attorney and former PD himself, rising to some fame as a result of his work on a case that became the subject of a 2009 movie called *The Informant!* starring Matt Damon. The film tells the overlapping stories of a massive price-fixing scandal in the early 1990s at the Archer-Daniels-Midland Company, a Fortune 100 company headquartered in Chicago, and an ADM executive (played by Damon) who was recruited as an FBI informant on the antitrust matter but was then found to be embezzling money from his employer during the investigation. Not wanting to destroy their antitrust case, the FBI and DOJ realized that their informant needed his own criminal defense lawyer, and they brought Epstein on to defend him. Prior to filming, the director Steven Soderbergh came to our courtroom to get a personal recollection of key details from Judge Epstein, producing a buzz of excitement of the kind that would be expected in any workplace if a famous director visited for the purpose of interviewing a coworker because that colleague was going to be a character in a major film.

In real life, Judge Epstein was married to a former prosecutor whose father was one of the most powerful trial attorneys in Chicago. The father, Philip Corboy, was such a successful legal figure that the street on which Chicago's City Hall and the Daley Center Civil Court complex are located is named the Honorary Philip H. Corboy Way. His daughter, the late Honorable Joan Corboy, became a judge at a fairly young age, perhaps partly due to the influence her father had in the right circles. I had the opportunity to work in her courtroom when I was just an intern, learning from the APDs who were assigned there that she was a heavy sentencer with a clear pro-State bent, but fair enough to allow defense wins that met her particular criteria. The mix of family power, success, and budding fame before the age of fifty must have been exhilarating, but the vagaries of life didn't care. Judge Corboy was killed in a freak accident when her arm or her clothing became stuck in an automatic gate in a parking garage at the family vacation condo in Florida. Several people heard her screaming for help as she was dragged and trapped between the gate and a wall, and a rescue attempt was made, but her injuries were grievous enough that she lapsed into a coma for several days before passing away. From what I heard, her father used his connections to have Judge Epstein appointed to the bench in the courtroom next to where his wife had presided, and the chambers adjacent to hers as well, to allow him to continue his prodigious legal career while trying to balance the burdens of caring for their children as a new widower.

Perhaps owing to the combination of intellect and pain that he carried, Judge Epstein quickly developed a reputation as being practically insufferable on the bench. The veterans in our office who were initially excited for the opportunity to work before one of our own were swiftly disillusioned by the judge's biting tone. So many of them refused the assignment that our bosses, one of whom had been Epstein's courtroom partner years before, could not find anyone willing to accept a permanent posting to work with him. Presented with the opportunity to get any sort of assignment in the Felony Trial Division literally years before my peers, and to gain the kind of experience that could only come from daily interaction with one of the very best and brightest—despite the enormous discrepancy between my responsibilities and my pay—I jumped at the chance to take one for the team, and my bosses allowed it. Judge Epstein called my supervisor, his former PD Homicide Task Force partner Frank Marino, and lodged a forceful protest: "You're sending me a kid? A *rookie!*?" Informed of the consequences of his rather vituperative judicial demeanor on our office's ability to find sacrificial lambs to go before him, the judge conditionally relented, and my career in the Felony Trial Division was born.

My assignment there lasted about four years, during which I litigated hundreds of cases and resolved thousands more. One memorable resolution came as the result of a plea conference that included the judge, a prosecutor, a probation officer, Ralph, and me, as we all discussed the details of a plea agreement for a woman charged with shoplifting. She was a repeat offender, and although the value of the stolen items was high enough to earn felony status, it was still a relatively low dollar amount. Nevertheless, her recidivist status made her eligible for tougher sentencing than she otherwise would have been, and the State wanted prison.

The sentencing range was five years at the top end, but there were still options for a non-penitentiary sentence at the judge's discretion. I had Ralph there to suggest several programs that might accept her, depending on what type of conditions the judge decided to impose. Probation officers couldn't be counted on to offer helpful alternatives if they didn't want the burden, and the prosecution was pushing to keep things simple with a two- or three-year bid, which they considered generous in light of her record. Judge Epstein put me on the spot to justify our request for leniency. I told him that in addition to the substance abuse problems that we saw so commonly, and her history of being in an abusive relationship that she couldn't easily escape without hurting her child, there was the fact that she was adopted by a foster family at a very young age. The adoption was confirmed by the pre-sentencing report prepared by the Probation Department, as were certain details about the ways in which her family situation had been very tough for her. My point was that she originally started on her downward spiral through no fault of her own, not by any choices she had made for herself.

The judge said, "So she was adopted, so what? Shouldn't she be over it by now?" I was really hit by what I saw as a callous lack of human understanding, and it struck a nerve with me personally. It's standard practice to take a deferential tone with judges as a nod to the respect they have earned and the simple reality that we need to work with them closely for the benefit of many clients. But I snapped: "What about your wife's death? Are you 'over it' by now?" I tried to make my point that there are some things that we don't "get over"; they become part of us instead, resurfacing in unpredictable ways that have to be managed, which is a skill set that some of us are better at than others. This woman stole some clothing. How the hell would prison help her break that pattern of behavior? Who are we really protecting? Her chance to get better seemed more valuable than a few overpriced items off the racks of some swanky department store.

Just about everyone in the room thought I had guaranteed my client the penitentiary with that outburst. Ralph even started moving his chair away from mine so that he wouldn't get drawn into the crossfire he was expecting. But Judge Epstein knew I was adopted, and he showed an aspect of his genuine wisdom, a crucial element of which is patient willingness to reconsider. He agreed to give my client a "last chance" over the fuming objections of the State and the Probation Department. Ralph had a place in mind where she could get several types of counseling not too far from where she lived.

I don't know if the woman really changed after that and stayed out of trouble, or if she failed and relapsed, which was statistically the far more likely scenario. "Last chances" were sometimes the best outcomes we could hope for, and to get them we needed to investigate not just what happened, but why, and be prepared to provide some alternative solutions instead of just punishing people. Resolutions like that gave us the feeling that it was at least possible that we were making a difference, and trying to redeem ourselves in the process. Maybe that was true for Judge Epstein too.

IV. TRIALS

The most intense pressure that ate at me as a criminal defense attorney came from the split in reality that occurred depending on whether I won or lost a trial. It strains every boundary of expression and communication to even attempt to describe the difference between incarceration and freedom, and it defies all logic and reason to consider just how thin the line of separation between them can be. Especially if I thought I should win—which was not always the case at the outset of the battle, but was almost always an idea I could latch on to somewhere along the way—then defeat was really devastating. Crying on the floor of the lockup is not a good look for any lawyer, but I've been there, and I can promise you that I'm not alone.

Protection of the accused is a noble concept, but it isn't charity. It's necessary because of the possibility of mistakes, farcical legal processes, and the weaponization of false accusations. Baseless or untrue allegations and sham trials are common enough features of corrupt systems, especially in societies with a power elite and a proletarian populace, that procedural protections and the jury system were conceived and implemented as democratic protection of the weak. As a public defender, it's a special badge of American pride to work for the government and against the government at the same time. We work to try to counteract State abuses; that's our contribution, and that's really all we can do.

Generally speaking, American law grants criminal defendants the right to choose between two forms of trial: one where the evidence is heard and the verdict decided by a judge alone, called a bench trial, and an alternative right to demand that the prosecution present the evidence against them publicly to twelve citizens who vote on the question of guilt or innocence, called a jury trial. There are exceptions for extremely minor crimes and extremely major ones (think relatively minor traffic offenses, on the one hand, and terrorism cases against certain non-citizens, on the other), and there may be additional exceptions from state to state, but a good rule of thumb is that if a person is facing the possibility of jail or prison, then they have the right to trial by bench or jury.

Most cases simply never get to any kind of hearing or trial due to plea agreements. In civil cases, cost containment and the certainty of negotiated outcomes dictate settlements most of the time, and there is a similar corollary in criminal court. Among the cases that do get to trial, there is an old unwritten rule floating around Cook County defense practitioners: Take winners to a bench, take losers to a jury. This is because there are relatively few cases that pass prosecutorial review and yet still have some clearly plausible theory of defense. When that does happen, attorneys will generally prefer to rely on the legal expertise and the professional objectivity of a judge to hear them. Judges still have a significant role in jury trials in terms of deciding what evidence will be allowed and conducting the trial itself, but the jury has the job of "trier of fact," meaning they have the power to decide what to believe and whether to convict or acquit. The reason that jury trials are such a tempting option for the defense is that the defendant cannot be convicted unless the jury's vote is unanimous, meaning that if we can convince even one juror that there is a reasonable doubt of the defendant's guilt, we win. It's a very polite understatement to say that some people will surprise you with what they are willing to believe or not; a less-guarded statement is that some people are credulous idiots, and they might be your only hope.

Our system of laws has many protections built in to ensure protection of the innocent, some of which are technical, and some of which are weak, but the right to a jury trial is both a very powerful check against arbitrary abuse of power, and usually irresistible theater too.

Watching legal dramas on television or in the movies might give someone the impression that trials are very common, but the reality is the exact opposite—jury trials are exceedingly rare, even for the prosecutors and public defenders whose daily routine revolves around courtroom hearings. "Heaters" (cases with intense public pressure) usually have to go to juries. If there is media or police emphasis on a particular case or defendant, a fact of human nature that lies at the junction of jurisprudence and self-preservation is that most judges instinctively protect their own position and reputation, whether they make that choice consciously or subconsciously. There are times when judges will tell the defense attorney that he or she will not get a good outcome from them and should not try. They can do this point-blank, or via hints and clues, but either way the message is unmistakable: pick twelve.

The inverse message is known as a "jury tax." I've also heard it referred to as the "How Dare You" tax and the "Asshole Penalty." Judges have been known to sentence defendants more harshly after a jury loss than they would have if the defendant had pleaded guilty. This is justified by using sentencing factors called aggravation and mitigation. The idea is that if someone pleads guilty, they have acknowledged responsibility for their crime, and some credit should be given for that act. On the other hand, if there was a fairly plain case of guilt, and there is the sense that the defendant chose not to acknowledge that and instead chose to waste time and resources, or was playing games with the emotions or personal schedules of victims or witnesses, then that is considered to be aggravating and justifies additional punishment.

Jury trials take days, or longer; they are a sort of journey taken together by the parties, involving some exposure of individual personalities, mixed in with professional interaction that we go to great lengths to dress up in formality, all with fairly high stakes in terms of intellect, ego, and, of course, punishment. As a lawyer in a jury trial in criminal court, you can usually tell if you've won or lost by whether or not the jurors look at you as they reenter the courtroom after their deliberations. It's not an exact science, but experience has taught me that they won't look at you if you've lost, unless they're just unable to look away due to some irresistible gravity of celebrity or disgust. When you've won, their eyes meet yours the moment they come through that door. Some try to keep a poker face, glancing away to focus on any piece of the floor or furniture that they can use as a brace. Either way, they know the answer, and they can barely contain themselves as their faces and body language betray them.

One of the ways in which the constitutional principle of presumption of innocence is protected during the pageantry of a jury trial is to allow defendants to wear street clothes whenever the jury sees them, to avoid the powerful visual cue of inmate clothing (aka "loser pajamas") that suggests this person belongs in jail. Some of the truly indigent clients of the Public Defender's Office don't have presentable clothes for a jury trial, so each Cook County branch office keeps a closet with donated coats, ties, shirts, and pants. These are exactly the kind of charity pieces that you might expect from the bottom of the barrel at Goodwill or the Salvation Army. These clothes are part of the presentation we are trying to make on behalf of our client, so they're chosen with as much care as possible under the circumstances. But when we're faced with a situation where we are being forced to go to trial against our best advice and we have the overwhelming sense that a jury tax is coming, there is a sort of coping mechanism that we indulge in that takes the form of a joke that the defendant doesn't need the closet, he needs to be fitted for a spacesuit, because at sentencing he's going to get launched.

Trials in general, and jury trials in particular, reduce the entire governmental prosecution and persecution enterprise to a competition to be the most reasonable party, as demonstrated on the record, in the public eye. As the lead defense attorney in a jury trial, you are trying to form a bond of trust with the jurors over the course of the proceedings. You need to display enough confidence and stewardship of the proceedings to gain respect from the jurors, despite the fact that you are definitely not in charge, and you are working against the same effort by the prosecution. The State always has the advantage of *gravitas*, of being presumed to be the so-called good guys, and your client is in the center of the bull's-eye of presumed bad guy. Sure, Americans have been told that a person is innocent until proven guilty, but that's mere lip service and polite theoretical academics. In reality, it's an almost universal instinct to think that the defendant wouldn't have gotten arrested if he or she hadn't done anything wrong.

Presenting the defense begins from the moment the pool of potential jurors walks into the room for the selection process. People judge by what they see, and that tendency is so powerful that there is no way around it and no reasonable basis to pretend otherwise. There is no guarantee that people will perceive you in some uniform way, but within certain stereotypes there is significant continuity. It is not polite to say it out loud, but it is absolutely true that we are all judged on our gender, age, race, pulchritude, and physical condition with regard to girth, height, or disability. This is especially true in professional settings like court, where other people's lives are in the hands of an empowered counsel. We cannot control perception, but what we can control is our presentation of grooming and attire; judgments of these are instantaneous and defining. Taken all together, a wealth of information is communicated literally in the blink of an eye, and it presents an image that cannot be undone, only augmented or confused. As defense counsel, you don't want to create more tides that you need to swim against than there already are. The more you can funnel people toward approval, the better. It's best done subtly, so they get the feeling that they are arriving at these opinions by themselves.

Jury selection begins with questionnaire forms that each citizen completes upon arrival at the courthouse for jury duty. These cover demographic basics that also speak volumes when properly interpreted: each person's age, address, educational background, job, and marital and family status are just the starting points. The State goes much further, running each potential juror through various databases of law-enforcement information, which enables them to see arrest histories, traffic citations, and credit scores. This gives them insight into who might have negative feelings about the police or be disinclined toward various societal norms and controls. Advanced research includes social media checks, because many people have posted or commented about political issues or causes. This is a window into behavior and speech that can be deeply revealing since people are speaking out voluntarily and are therefore much more comfortable and authentic in their messaging. Public defenders don't get anywhere near this level of information, leaving us to request a certain latitude from the presiding judge to allow us to ask questions of each person based on their answers on the questionnaire. Most people hate being questioned in public, but it's the best system we have to get some insights about preconceived notions or potential biases.

It's a commonly joked-about phenomenon that people will come up with any number of bizarre and nakedly selfish excuses to get out of jury duty. These halfhearted pleas of inconvenience aren't unexpected, so it's wrong to say we are surprised to hear them, but some people are so unabashed in their entitlement that there is always a sense of renewed, exasperated disbelief on the part of judges and trial lawyers to hear some of the things people will try to float as reasons they should be excused. Especially in light of that aspect of human nature that has been laid bare by the existence of social media and the twitching eagerness some people have to share any thought or opinion that pops into their heads as though it could somehow be popularly significant or persuasive, you would think that people would be genuinely excited to seize what could be the single greatest—possibly only—opportunity of their lives to exercise real power. Instead, we hear a laundry list of work and childcare-related inconveniences, peppered with the occasional example of someone who has likely been coached to say some outlandish nonsense about being incurably racist or emotionally and intellectually overcome with bias.

The ultimate decision to take a case to trial doesn't rest with the attorney; it's entirely up to the defendant. We can and do make strong recommendations, but the final word is theirs alone, which means there can be disagreements even about this most critical choice. Private attorneys who are being paid for their counsel have the option of withdrawing from the case if they and their clients are in conflict about essential strategy, but public defenders don't have that choice—we have to be on board either way, whether we are driving the bus or just along for the ride. We have some clients who aren't interested in going to trial even if there is a decent chance to do so, simply because it will take too long to get there. On the other end of the strategic spectrum are those hardened souls who have no plausible defense but still refuse to try to minimize the damage by pleading out.

In my experience, the cases where this kind of crap happened the most were burglary charges. Statutory precision notwithstanding, burglary is the act of entering into private property with the intent to commit a theft once inside. Chicago is flooded with cases of general burglary, burglary to auto, and burglary to residence. The homeless and the poor collect these charges like a magnet collects iron, so there aren't any veteran Cook County public defenders in the Felony Trial Division who haven't had thousands of burglary cases. The thing is that for sentencing purposes, someone's first or second burglary conviction usually doesn't bring a very harsh sentence. First-timers will probably get probation, and second-timers will probably get a relatively light prison sentence that they can finish quickly with credit for pretrial detention and good behavior. But third convictions carry the punishment of recidivist sentencing, so those defendants are treated as "Class X" offenders, meaning a mandatory prison sentence between six and thirty years. Whatever the logic of increasing punishments for repeat offenses may be, the people who are subject to them are stuck on a different kind of logic altogether—the kind that prevents them from wrapping their minds around the idea of getting a much more severe punishment than they received in the past for the exact same conduct on each occasion.

Those defendants have been sitting in the county jail during their pretrial detention, watching a steady stream of prisoners with the same charges as they have, but who are able to take pleas and walk out the door. They are absolutely convinced that they deserve the same outcome. When that Class X offer is presented, even for the minimum of six years, they respond with angry denial. This proves to them that their PDs are failures who are idiots at best, and traitors to their cause at worst, and they fall back on the advice of the frequent fliers who consider themselves jailhouse lawyers. That wisdom has produced the following familiar lockup refrain: "I'm not gonna take that time, they're gonna have to give it to me."

When you do have one of those most cantankerous clients who cannot be persuaded by logic, reason, threats, or the time-tested favorite of a collective browbeating by the line assistant and his or her partners and supervisors, that's when you need to get creative with your opening statements and closing arguments. You can't just stand up and say the truth: "I have no idea what the defense is. I advised against doing this at all, but this asshole is making me do it." So you pull together your straightest face and pour out some claptrap about the requirement of proof being "beyond a reasonable doubt" and how the State will fail to meet their burden. Depending on the ass-kicking you take after that, and on whether your client has been just a stubborn fool or a pernicious prick, closing arguments present an opportunity to take free license to indulge your inner Al Pacino and let loose whatever it is that the lawyer has always wanted to say but has been too afraid to say it. One of the unwritten rules of trials is that the judge is trying to make sure to avoid errors that could be used as the basis for an appeal. They don't like the blot on their record of being reversed, so they tend to afford wider latitude to defense arguments than they would otherwise allow, just to deprive the defendant of the chance to claim that his lawyer was muzzled. PDs all have some hilarious stories about arguments they've made or heard about when someone with nothing to lose went full tinfoil hat and started ranting about evidence that wasn't presented and how it relates to the flag, Cuban cigars, or GPS trackers in our cell phones. I admit that doesn't really help our reputations overall, but if we're at that point anyway and are forbidden from being transparent about how we got there, well, some say laughter is the best medicine, and we just might need to take a dose.

In the midst of one such jury trial I had where my client walked into a construction site and stole tools from a truck in full view of about a dozen workers, only to be arrested with the proceeds about a block away from the scene a very short time later, I discovered that the arresting officers had taken some handwritten notes with the initial description of the offender provided by the witnesses. Those notes were never given to us as part of the pretrial discovery process, despite the clear legal requirement to do so, which is not only a constitutional and statutory requirement, but also enforced by court rules. Both the State's Attorney's Office and the Public Defender's Office have boilerplate motions for discovery that track the language of the applicable laws and rules. Officially requesting all police reports, documents, and notes as part of pretrial discovery is so standard, such a bedrock of daily practice ritual, that anyone would be hard-pressed to find a single case where such a request wasn't made. In this case, as is almost always true with initial descriptions, the information was imprecise and wrong about a particular article of clothing. Having almost nothing else to use, I seized on the chance to argue for a mistrial on the basis of withheld evidence.

Denying my motion as swiftly and forcefully as he could, the judge pointed out that I had failed to issue subpoenas to the arresting officers personally that would have served as additional obligations for the production of those notes. His point wasn't that I had no right to them, nor that I hadn't followed proper procedure to obtain them, but that I hadn't been as entirely thorough as possible. Rather than accepting his advice as a lesson from a well-intentioned mentor, I engaged in a stubborn argument that my motion for discovery and my reliance on well-established law were more than good enough. Our back-and-forth escalated to the point where we were shouting at each other, which only ended when the judge finally ordered me to sit down and shut up or be held in direct contempt. Choosing to flee the scene instead, I ducked into the Clerk's Office adjacent to the courtroom and was followed by the lead prosecutor, with whom I had an excellent working relationship. She said: "What the hell are you doing? Are you nuts? Why are you pissing him off on a case like this?!" To which I replied, "*Because* it's a case like this. You gotta let me have my fun."

We lost, and my client took his sentence right on the chin. But several members of his family were in attendance and had seen the fight I put up in a losing cause; their expressions of gratitude were among the nicest comments I ever received on the job.

Another absolute truth about trials is that there is always an element of unpredictability. This is a logical concession that I think all professionals have to make when telling a client that particular outcomes are almost never absolutely certain, despite whatever avalanche of evidence is pointing to an otherwise obvious result. I wasn't the lead counsel on the trial that comes to mind to best illustrate this point, instead, I was in the position called "second chair," just assisting to lighten the first chair's workload and add a trial stat to my résumé. The case was what we call a "caught inside" burglary, where the offender was literally arrested while still inside the scene of the crime. There is very little leeway for the defense to argue that the cops got the wrong guy in a case like that, but the client was flat-out refusing to plead, so off to trial we went.

The State put the victim/property owner on the stand for the purpose of establishing that he had not given the defendant permission to enter his garage, and to identify the man whom he'd found there and had arrested. When the moment came for that most dramatic of courtroom scenes where they ask the witness to point to the offender and make the essential identification, the guy said, "The man at the defense table wearing the glasses." Well, there were three of us at the defense table who were men wearing glasses, so they asked him to try again. "The man at the defense table wearing the necktie." Again, three for three. Slightly exasperated, they pressed on: "Can you please be more specific?" "Sure, the black guy." At least he finally nailed something unique. After the jury walked him and we got our FNG (finding of not guilty), the prosecutors weren't even mad. One of the jurors told me the ASA's eye roll upon hearing the witness resort to the race card was the moment she'd made up her mind.

Sometimes the combination of credit for pretrial detention and the inevitability of a prison sentence for a conviction combine to help us persuade an otherwise scared defendant that taking the risk of trial is actually worth the gamble. When they know they're going down without a miracle, offering them at least a fighting chance can look pretty appealing. I had a client with a gun possession case who was a bit older than the norm, somewhere around his mid-thirties, who had a record from his younger years but who'd managed to keep himself out of trouble for the better part of a decade since his last transgression. Despite the provable changes he'd undergone to become a different, better person since his last offense—such as finishing his degree, getting married, having children, and resolving his substance abuse issues—he was being treated as a repeat offender.

He was facing a stiff prison bid that would derail his new life for at least half a decade if he were convicted. He was the kind of client we ache to help, and his story about the gun only made me all the more eager to dig deep.

The gun belonged to his friend who legally possessed the requisite license from the State of Illinois called a Firearm Owner's Identification Card (a "FOID card," for short), and thus legally owned the gun. They had been to a firing range in some distant suburb, then drove back to the city to go home. The gun was being transported in a secure firearm transport box in the trunk of the car, which was both safe and compliant with applicable law. On their way back downtown, they called my client's wife to come meet them for lunch at a spot near where they all lived, after which the friends planned to part ways. My client's wife walked to the designated restaurant to meet them, since they had taken her car for the trip, but she changed her mind about where she wanted to eat before they arrived.

For some dumb reason that I'll never understand, while they were parked on a public way in the city of Chicago, the man who owned the gun decided that was the proper time and place to just make sure it wasn't still loaded from their time at the range, and he went to the trunk, opened it, took the gun out of the box, and inspected it. There was no allegation that the gun was being used to threaten anyone, or even that any specific crime was being committed (since gun possession can be perfectly legal), but some anonymous citizen called 911 to report seeing two guys "waving a gun around on the street," and that was exactly the kind of call to merit an immediate police response. The cops arrived so fast that although there had been time to put the gun back in the box, and time for my client's wife to sit in the passenger seat to wait, the two men were still standing there discussing whether it was worth it to go somewhere else to eat or if they should just bag it and make plans for some other time, when the police pulled up.

All the witnesses agreed on several key points. From the moment the police were on the scene, the gun was in the box inside the car, and not in anyone's hands. Moreover, the gun was legally registered to the friend, and the car was legally registered to the wife. The testimony diverged from there, although about only one detail: all three civilians said the gun box was in the trunk, but the police said it was sitting on the back seat "in plain view." That difference had a legal significance that only the police understood; since the entire interaction was predicated on an anonymous tip, and since the police had no warrant to search the car or arrest anyone connected to it, their alleged observation was the only basis they had to search the car and ultimately arrest my client. Once they "found" the gun and ran everyone's backgrounds, they used that information and the allegation in the 911 call to charge my client.

Believing this was a clear case of fabricated probable cause, I filed a pretrial motion to have the search and subsequent arrest deemed unconstitutional. To my bitter disappointment, the judge chose to believe the police testimony and denied my motion. That left me in the sorry state of not only having lost a motion I fervently believed that I deserved to win, but also significantly reduced my leverage in any potential plea discussions, and with a client who now doubted the overall reliability of my counsel. If we did go to trial, the judge had already decided that my best witnesses—the gun owner who was perfectly willing to testify that the gun was his and it was being transported legally—was actually a liar. Doing the quick math on just how completely screwed we were, we requested a date for a jury trial and went about figuring out a new strategy.

Only on the eve of trial did it really dawn on me that the police and prosecution had also been focused on the pretrial maneuvering and may have overlooked, as I initially did, the fact that there was a flaw in their proof that my client had ever possessed the gun. They couldn't use the anonymous call at trial because that witness was never located. Since that person would not be in court to testify, what they had reported to 911 was hearsay. Without anyone who could say that the defendant had even touched the gun, in order to prove possession of the weapon, the prosecution was relying on the fact that both the defendant and the gun had been in the car together at the same time. In fact, his friend had admitted that during the hearing on the pretrial motion. But motion evidence and trial evidence are not the same thing; the State would need to prove the defendant's presence in the car at trial. Realizing that crucial element of their case would fail if the State just stuck to calling their officers—if the officers stuck to their previous testimony, and if my client shut up and didn't testify at all—on the day of the trial we waived the jury and went with a bench, and I sat back and waited like a buzzard.

Sure enough, the State got complacent based on the pretrial testimony and the fact that the defendant's wife was in the passenger seat, suggesting that my client had driven there and just gotten out before the police arrived. I never even questioned them on that point, I just let them plow ahead. The sweetest part of winning that case was interrupting the judge as he was in the middle of explaining why he was about to convict my client. When he got to the part about how the defendant had clearly been driving the car, I cut him off with a Columbo-esque "Now wait just a minute, Your Honor . . ." and pointed out the assumption. The trial proof was that the gun was in the car, the car was registered to the wife, and the defendant was arrested on the sidewalk. The judge's face and voice contorted; I could actually see the moment he realized that I was right. The State moved to reopen their case but were denied. Having pulled out a victory from the jaws of defeat, back in the lockup the defendant gave me the kind of hug you only get after saving a man's life. The sheriff's deputy made sure to sour the moment: "Get your ass on the elevator. If you two want to give each other reach-arounds, you can do it on your own time."

Before any trial, the defense is professionally expected to interview all the potential witnesses to take their statements, to ensure that their testimony doesn't improve with time and that they don't contradict themselves at trial. In the most difficult cases, this means we are going to talk to the victims themselves, or their surviving family members, or to police officers, in an attempt to get statements from the people who are most hostile to our clients and, by extension, to us. It's a highly delicate endeavor. They aren't legally required to speak to us and certainly don't feel compelled by etiquette to be kind in their refusals. My first chief supervisor in the office, the brilliant but understated Mr. Gino Peronti, and my primary investigator Ralph Metz were two of the most experienced practitioners around, and they taught me that our role is to check every possible defense, paper it all up, be aware that the record is our only ally, and do the best we can to protect our clients' rights. It helps to shift mindsets a bit and think of ourselves as defenders of the process, with the Constitution as our true client.

Even before the Illinois Supreme Court established the Capital Litigation Trial Bar and its additional requirements for attorneys to be allowed to handle cases with the most severe possible punishment, the Cook County Public Defender's Office recognized the need for concentrated practice groups comprised of the most experienced lawyers who would have access to better resources than usual to meet the challenges of complex cases. We weren't able to create a vast range of task forces like the police and prosecution have done, but we had specialist units in addition to the Felony Trial Division attorneys, including a Forensic Science Division, Juvenile Justice specialists, appellate lawyers, at least one PD who had carved out a niche representing clients with severe mental illnesses, and the most elite group in our office, the Homicide Task Force.

Young attorneys in the office seek opportunities to advance, and to get to the higher pay grades required a mix of union-regimented seniority and breadth of professional experience. The specialist units generally had a higher concentration of their cases go to trial, so one method of accruing stats was to volunteer to assist whenever there was a case with enough legwork to go around. The lead attorney on a given case is referred to as the "first chair," and there can be an unlimited number of assisting PDs as may be necessary. That's how I got a taste for what may come if I were to stay in the office and could make it to the Homicide Task Force. I suppose it's understandable to be curious about the outer limits of human depravity. Based on that instinct, every criminal defense attorney is asked about the very worst case of their careers or that they know of.

Here is mine: Two teenagers were dating each other but were unmarried, and they had an unwanted baby. Owing to some combination of fear and ignorance, they were unable or unwilling to surrender their parental rights through legal channels. Whether the baby died as the result of abuse or neglect could not be precisely scientifically ascertained, and that would form the essential trial issue, together with a dispute between the two of them concerning principal culpability. Any unnatural death of a child, particularly a baby, is poignant and disturbing; that alone would have been enough to set this case apart. But it was the manner of the disposal of the remains that led to the detection of the crime, and haunted anyone who saw the evidence.

The corpse had been dismembered, the parts then buried in shallow holes behind the home of a family member. That household had a dog who dug up several limbs and chewed them, but not to the point of total destruction. Seeing the remnants of the carcass lying about the yard, the decision was made to unearth all the remains and soak them in a bucket of battery acid. That also failed to completely eliminate the evidence, so they resorted to simpler means: they asked their neighbors if they could borrow a blender, which they used in an attempt to purée the remaining bits of tissue and bone. After all of that, the residual sludge of what had once been a human being was flushed down the toilet.

The neighbors realized that they had not seen the baby in some time, and their questions about its whereabouts were answered vaguely and curtly. They requested the return of their appliance, and the blender was washed and returned. However, the owners immediately noticed a putrid odor coming from the inner mechanism and took it apart for a deeper clean. Upon close inspection, splintered bone and shredded tissue were unmistakable.

When arrested, each parent initially denied knowledge of the whereabouts of the baby, then blamed the other for the child's demise. The prosecution realized some evidentiary weaknesses and promptly offered a deal to the mother to flip against the father. She took it and gave a statement that incriminated him in the strangulation killing of the infant and the subsequent efforts to destroy the proof. It was our job to raise sufficient doubt about his guilt, principally by accusing her of being motivated by self-preservation to pin it all on him, while being guilty at the least of being the worst conceivable mother and being obviously equally complicit in whatever had befallen her child.

In murder cases, the prosecution almost always begins the presentation of their case with a witness who is called to establish "Proof of Life" for the deceased, the last person to see the victim alive, or a parent or other close family member. Technically, the purpose is to establish that the person had been alive before a certain date or event, but in practice, it serves as a highly emotional opening act in the drama of the State's case. In this case it would be the maternal grandmother, and time of death was a key issue that could not be precisely established, so we had to talk to her. One of the things you learn with experience is that people react to tragedies and stressors in different and sometimes unpredictable ways. The State loves to second-guess people's actions and judge them on some removed scale of reasonability, always arguing about what a "reasonable" or "innocent" person would do, should have done, must've known, could have thought, and so on. It's wildly speculative and ignorant of the true scope of human reactions—some would even say self-righteous and racist—but they work hard to make it seem like the essence of reasonability.

We didn't have the kind of torturous pretrial interviews that are required in cases where we are trying to ascertain if someone is wrong or lying. The first chair handled the cops in a pretrial motion to suppress the statement on the grounds of involuntariness. The medical examiner was clear on paper that it was impossible to determine the cause and manner of death. The co-defendant had her own attorneys, who forbade us from interviewing her. The neighbors were all too happy to talk. The only really difficult person was the co-defendant's mother, who was around forty-five years old and was extremely protective of her daughter as opposed to our client, as could be easily expected. She lathered us with venom, but some of her points were fair enough as they aligned with the State's case: this didn't have to happen if they really didn't want the child. There were options to give the child away. If it had been an accident, there was the obvious option and requirement to call for help. To her, the defendant was just trying to erase something that was disruptive to his life. But that "something" was a human being, and the destruction of that human being was an act of criminal depravity; the destroyer needed to pay the price.

Our defense was that there was a lack of concrete proof as to what specifically happened, and it could've just as easily been an accident that was followed by a panicked and tragically grotesque type of burial. We focus-tested how to describe the acts that were done to the remains, using "disposal," "removal," "concealment," and versions of "getting rid of." That went . . . poorly. We knew the State would hammer us with all kinds of colorful language to maximize the brutality, so we went with "burial" even though it was generously euphemistic (to say the least), to try to counterbalance their bloody descriptions with some respect. We genuinely believed that there was insufficient proof to convict. The jury did not see it our way. Those ultra-close-up pictures of what was found in the blender were just too much. Frankly, knowing that this kind of suffering is entirely human-made, and that this type of behavior is some combination of learned sadism and inherent defect, it will break you.

How do public defenders handle cases like that? While the head-line grabbers are relatively rare, for every heater in the public eye, there are thousands that are just as miserable and heartbreaking on an interpersonal level. We are the ones who are appointed to shep-herd those cases through the process where there is no defense, where the actions of the defendant are legally and morally indefen-sible, and the outcome is an inevitable, if drawn-out, formality. We end up in a type of cold war with our own clients—in addition to suf-fering the smoldering wrath of the victims, police, prosecutors, and other observers—just for being "on his side." I dare suggest that most defense attorneys struggle with extreme cases and defendants, with the process of interviewing witnesses in preparation for trial, with incessant losing, with devastating sentencing hearings and victim impact statements, and with the disapprobation of society and our peers. What we see is that in many cases, these horrific outcomes didn't have to happen if the humanity of the criminal had been rec-ognized, acknowledged, built, or cherished at an earlier age. The FBI has spent an enormous amount of time and resources studying causes of criminality and behavioral patterns, and they once had a theory that 5 percent of people are genuinely good people seeking to do good deeds, 5 percent are truly evil who seek to do harm, and 90 percent of the entire population are followers who will behave in the manner they are led one way or the other. As PDs, we think about the contrast in experiences between someone who has had it good and someone who has had it bad, and the myriad and maddeningly unprovable ways that bad luck and bad people are formed.

It takes a special soul to manage the strain and emotions that need to be endured to do the job professionally. I have to readily admit that I burned out before I had to handle the worst of the worst. I always thought I would be a career public defender, but I looked at the vet-erans in our office and I saw highly stressed people. I heard rumors of poor health, alcoholism, divorce. I saw how they were overworked, underpaid, and grossly unappreciated. The burdens of knowing you will lose an overwhelming amount of the time, and losing when you think you should absolutely win, and the human suffering all around, is all extremely difficult to endure. Just as the winning and adoration builds happiness and career momentum for the police and prosecution, the losing and constant disdain and contempt can crush PDs' spirits quite effectively. I remember our contracts expiring every two years, and the county dragging out negotiations over raises of 1 or 2 percent, sometimes for years at a time, so that we were working without formal contracts, and the dramatic contrast that was so plainly evident as patrolmen without college degrees arrived at the courthouse in their new Cadillacs and Corvettes, fresh from their lake cabins in Wisconsin.

Fortunately, defending those who are truly evil is extremely rare. As to the justification of being a defense attorney in general, when I was confronted by people who were offended by the notion of society providing assistance to those who are accused of harming it, I viewed it as a simplistic question, and I felt that I needed to respond in a way that was direct, appropriate, and capable of instant comprehension. I would posit that there are undeniably some innocents; maybe not many, but absolutely there are some. Once that is acknowledged— and it almost universally is—then the answer is simple too: if I want to be ready to do my absolute best to defend the truly innocent, then it helps to practice on a lot of guilty ones first.

V. DNA

Being a public defender is not a lucrative job. It may be a noble calling, but in terms of both pay and respect, it is very unrewarding. In
the movie *Lethal Weapon 4*, comedian Chris Rock plays a streetwise
cop who's always ready with a snappy quip, and in the course of making an arrest that represents the quintessential "good guy gets the
bad guy" movie moment, he recites a very cinematic version of the
Miranda warning that references public defenders in a taunt: "You
have the right to an attorney. If you can't afford an attorney, we will
provide you with the *dumbest fucking lawyer on earth*!" It stung. And
the reason it stung was because it reduced our entire profession to
a cruel joke. The generalization of public defenders as bad lawyers
is as true as a generalization can be, which is to say it isn't factually
accurate at all, but it is definitely centered on an element of common experience. We had many lawyers in the office who were not
interested in reading constant legal updates. We had many who
were not invested in delving into intricate details about procedures
or even case facts. We had many who were not intellectually curious
about the roots of criminal jurisprudence, its evolution, the roads
that have been tested and closed, and the paths that remain open
to those with imagination and spirit. Somehow we even had many
with poor senses of hygiene and personal presentation. We certainly
had plenty who weren't there to fight for freedom, but because that's
where the flotsam and jetsam of lawyers wash up, and for the rela-

tively stress-free niche that can be carved out in a unionized job with no profit motive and no performance incentive.

As much as it would be nice to think that people are attracted to careers in law out of a recognition that justice is essential for a functioning society, let alone one that strives to be egalitarian, the fact of the matter is that many people are attracted to it on the simple basis of earning potential. Some sectors of the legal world pay incredibly high salaries and offer opportunities for bonuses and awards that can provide regal, multigenerational wealth. Undergraduate and law students are aware of these possibilities. Part of the American academic experience is framed as a competition with other students to be top of the class, to be admitted to elite schools and selected for prestigious programs, all as a sort of premarket crucible to filter out the ones who lack the taste for earning and filter up the ones who possess it with a killer instinct. After all, we are only as valuable to our masters as the numbers bear out.

There is a joke that floats around Chicago legal circles that goes something like this: The University of Chicago trains judges; Northwestern trains big-firm partners; Loyola, DePaul, and Kent train La Salle Street litigators; and John Marshall (now UIC) trains grunts. Those of us who studied at JMLS generally found ourselves there as a function of trying to fight our way into a profession that didn't necessarily believe we were going to make it. Our reputation was that we represented the bottom rung of the Chicago legal scene, and we knew it. To be quite honest, I went to law school primarily because it was a path my parents approved of, I didn't know what else to do after college, and the thing that brought me the most joy and success in high school was being on the debate team. When a young person is in law school, there are some very different paths that can be pursued in terms of practice fields, and when my friends and family urged me to prioritize future earnings and choose an area of focus that could bring big paydays, I was initially receptive. However, big-firm jobs were flat out of reach, in addition to being lethally boring, so there was no point in trying to master the fields they covet most, such as corporate law, tax and estate planning, intellectual property, and contracts. The next best thing was to embrace the role of street-fighter, focus on the relatively level playing field of jury trials, and try to score by winning. So I took my first legal job at a firm that did bankruptcy, divorce, and torts. They were all about trying to take the biggest possible slice of judgments or settlements, and it didn't really matter if that money came from ambulance chasing or collecting a percentage of someone's major life failures. In all fairness I wasn't there for very long, but I can honestly say that I didn't learn much about the law there, except that those practice areas were the triumvirate of misery as far as I was concerned. I didn't even quit—I just left one day without taking my paycheck and never went back. From what I heard they weren't even upset, since it wasn't the first time that happened. Riding home on the Skokie Swift CTA train that night, I had the chance to talk to a classmate who was clerking at the local branch of the Cook County Public Defender's Office. She said they were practically desperate for help, and all I had to do was show up and offer. Since I was perfectly capable of meeting that criteria, and because actual litigation without the corruption of cash incentives seemed like the only refuge of sanity in the world I was reluctantly joining, I went.

My classmate wasn't kidding—they were desperate for help. The first day I went to the Skokie courthouse on Old Orchard Road, I was practically grabbed by a three-person team who worked one of the Felony Trial courtrooms on the Chicago side, as opposed to the suburban side. My duties would be to handle the calendar book, the old-fashioned way they kept track of case continuances and hearing dates, then help them with case reviews and research when we got back to the office. I was allowed to sit at the defense table in the well of the courtroom, and accompany them into the lockup to sit in on client meetings. It all felt so real, so important. I was absolutely besotted, and from that day on, I never really considered anything else.

Except once. As a junior in high school, I'd been the victim of a violent crime, although not exactly the stuff of headlines. A friend and I went to Northbrook Court for some last-minute gift shopping on Christmas Eve, and we were not alone. The parking lot was filled to capacity as a nighttime snowstorm began, piquing the holiday stress of the circling hunters on our deadline prowl. A guy who was waiting for a space saw one open up slightly behind him, where I was, and moved to force me to reverse so that he could enter. However, I couldn't back up even if I'd wanted to, because additional traffic had filled in the row behind me. Exchanging honks and gestures as one does in those sorts of encounters, he got out of his car and marched with purpose straight toward mine. Expecting an exchange of holiday greetings that might've rhymed with "go pluck yourself," I rolled down my window, only to be taught a tough lesson in the rules of road rage. He reached in and choked me for a good ten seconds, thrashing me around and cussing me out with the vigor of a drunken Bears fan after a Packers game.

He was arrested and sent to court in Skokie, and I was notified by the prosecution that my attendance was required as the complaining witness. I put on my Sunday best and prepared to enjoy the opportunity to face him again under vastly different circumstances, where he might not feel so free to be a raging bully and abuse a kid for his own convenience. Instead, some deal was worked out privately between whispering adults, following which he muttered some vague apology to the judge instead of to me and was sent on his merry way. Amid my confusion and slight disappointment, I remember thinking that the courthouse seemed like an excellent place to work, with its air of formality and solemnity, and the cordial pleasantries between the lawyers on both sides. The notion was vague at best, but then again so are most thoughts about future career paths in the minds of typical seventeen-year-olds like I was at the time.

That innocence turned out to be a fleeting luxury, a light that very soon would dim for me as it was extinguished entirely for someone I knew well.

During my freshman year in college, a kid I'd known in high school was murdered. His name was David Chereck, and he was a few years younger than I was, so he was still in high school when he died. I'd been his mentor on the Niles West Debate Team, a club whose most notable alumnus is US Attorney General Merrick Garland. David was strangled, and his body was dumped in a forest clearing just a few miles over from the 7-Eleven convenience store where he was last seen alive. Both sites were places I passed very regularly, as was the graveyard he was said to be cutting through when he happened to be confronted by the person or persons who killed him. His murder went unsolved for years, and for a long time it seemed like it would stay that way forever, leaving his family with an open wound of unanswered questions alongside their permanent scars of devastating loss. David's case lingered in my mind, planting seeds of doubt about the limits of investigative reach.

By the time I was in my second year of interning for the PD's Office and graduation was on the horizon, it had become clear that I was a good fit in criminal court. I'd won a few cases as a licensed student practitioner, I'd demonstrated excellent attention to detail and preparation that not all the interns for the State or PDs had managed, I was a very polished public speaker, and, frankly, I was clean-cut and could put on a decent suit. I really looked the part of eager attorney, and the ASAs came to me and said I should be on their side instead of wasting my time with the PDs. It made sense for a poli-sci major like me to at least explore the traditional path to power, and I figured it would give me the chance to work on cases like David's, so I agreed to prepare an application and submit to an interview.

The problem was that by then I had two years of experience reading police reports, going out on investigations, talking to defendants, listening to testimony, working side by side with the defense attorneys, and seeing how the system worked from the inside. It didn't take anything but the slightest amount of checking to see that the police were lying about *something* in an overwhelming number of cases, and yet the prosecutors reflexively and blindly defended them for the sake of their preferred form of order. Of course there are some

patriotic people who are prosecutors and cops, but whether by necessity or choice, they subscribe to a totally different set of ethics than I
do because they are perfectly willing to sacrifice an endless stream of
human beings on the altar of authoritarianism. I had a front-row seat
to watch the so-called war on drugs play out as a modern American
genocide. It was absurd propaganda to even call it a war on drugs. I
never ever saw a package of drugs held at gunpoint and handcuffed,
or dragged out of its car and beaten bloody, or threatened with false
charges for not being able to turn over a gun, or having its house torn
apart by a crew of renegades without the threat of any repercussions
whatsoever, or thrown in a cell with a hundred other people and denied protection from violence and communication with family and
lawyers, or given lengthy, life-destroying prison sentences for being
in possession of itself—but I saw all of that and more happening to
human beings nearly every single day. It was as though our so-called
leaders learned nothing from the disastrous calamity of Prohibition,
which was the very thing that made our city entirely synonymous
with gangsterism for nearly a century; or worse, they actually did
learn from it and decided to double down.

Then there were the most egregious injustices that have happened
in and around Chicago that "the system" was failing to address. The
first person in US history to have his conviction overturned by DNA
evidence was falsely convicted in Cook County, Illinois. His name
was Gary Dotson, who by most subsequent accounts was a totally
innocent kid who had the awful misfortune of being in the wrong
place at the worst possible time, which was the time and place where
a young woman decided to invent one of the worst possible kinds of
lies: a completely false rape accusation against a total stranger in order to cover up a pregnancy that resulted from a consensual act with
her boyfriend that she was too embarrassed to confess to her foster
parents. Dotson's plight was the subject of intense local interest and
media coverage before DNA evidence even existed—not because his
original case was so unusual, but because after he'd been convicted

and sat in prison for about five years and even lost his first appeal, the woman whose accusation and testimony were the bases for his arrest and conviction came forward to admit that she'd falsified the entire event. However, both the prosecutors and the original trial judge said they didn't believe her retraction and confession, and they refused to set Dotson free. Seemingly out of options in official tribunals, defense attorneys turned to a different institution of American power, the court of public opinion.

The public didn't need scientific or legal expertise to grasp the drama of a false rape conviction that the authorities refused to remedy, apparently on the sole basis of not wanting to admit they were duped by a sixteen-year-old girl who had inserted herself into the story line of a pulp-fiction fantasy novel called *Sweet Savage Love* to fabricate her claims. When the defendant's and the woman's lawyers succeeded in beating enough drums that the authorities were forced to do something, the governor orchestrated a totally unprecedented procedure where he himself presided over a televised clemency hearing that was held at the then-brand-new State of Illinois Center in the heart of the Loop. "Media circus" is a term without precise definition, but when the woman's dirty underwear was projected onto an enormous screen in juxtaposition with her salacious testimony about her sexual behavior, nobody needed academic delineation to understand what was going on.

Despite having lied and sent an innocent man to prison, the woman earned some public respect by trying to fix things and taking the heat of literally exposing herself in shame, only to experience a taste of what most defendants go through when all the relevant law-enforcement officials called her a liar and dismissed her claims. Governor James R. Thompson, himself a former prosecutor, manipulated the evidence at the clemency hearing via selective witness exclusion: he prohibited the testimony of Dr. Charles McDowell from the US Air Force Office of Special Investigations, who had conducted the largest scientific study of false rape allegations ever undertaken and created a twelve-point model of indicators. When witness testimony is not allowed in a trial or hearing, in order to preserve the issue for appeal, the side that wanted to call the witness offers a "proffer" instead, which is a detailed summary of what the testimony would have been if it had been permitted. That is how the record shows that Dr. McDowell would have testified that this case fit his model nearly perfectly, including scratches on the woman's stomach that showed a pattern of "cross-hatch superficial self-mutilation" that typifies false claims.

By the end of the clemency hearing, everyone knew that the evidence included an initial description of the alleged attacker that didn't match the defendant; a discredited prosecution forensic "expert" from the Illinois State Police who lied about his credentials to testify that evidentiary semen and hairs likely came from Dotson, even though he had a different blood type than the one identified in the samples; a highly respected federal investigator who had a detailed scientific model that demonstrated numerous ways the evidence fit a pattern of false accusations; and of course the retraction and pleas for absolution by the accuser herself. None of that was deemed persuasive, and Dotson's petition was rejected. His original conviction was in 1979, the hearing debacle occurred in 1985, and in 1988 DNA technology became available and irrefutably proved that Dotson was not the source of the "genetic material" collected after the alleged attack—it was from the boyfriend who'd knocked the girl up, just as she'd belatedly confessed. Unbelievably, the governor and the prosecution still resisted justice, taking the position that they remained opposed to "clemency" for an innocent man. They only begrudgingly relented in 1989, and even then they let the conviction sit on Dotson's record for an additional thirteen years! It wasn't until 2002 that Dotson was finally granted the acknowledgment of innocence he'd always deserved in the form of a full pardon from a different governor. Coming on the heels of the Greylord corruption scandal that exposed the bribery of judges in the Cook County criminal courts, and occurring nearly in parallel with two seismic unsolved nightmares in the Unabomber attacks and the Tylenol cyanide murders, the Dotson case was one of the major recurring news threads throughout the 1980s that concerned local criminal justice, or the lack thereof, showing the whole world that Chicago may have outlasted Capone, but could still be seen as a three-headed monster of corruption, incompetence, and cruelty.

DNA was just getting started with us. When the use of DNA evidence in criminal cases first became possible, I think both the prosecution and the defense immediately grasped that this was a division of our world into a before and after. My impression was that the police and prosecution believed that they were going to catch and convict every criminal on earth, and the defense bar feared that not only were we going to lose a lot more cases, but that the new level of certainty in identifying offenders would produce a corresponding "zero-tolerance"-style era of authoritarian punishments. DNA was fingerprints on steroids, a strength of evidence almost to the level of the voice of the Lord pointing down to individuals and saying "it was him." If this new technology could remove nearly all doubt on the question of guilt, it was easy to imagine that it would also remove any hesitation to drop the hammer of retribution that previously hinged on that doubt. What we were all just a step slower to grasp was the corollary strength DNA had to exonerate people, and the continued relevance of the simple old-fashioned ways that any system that relies on human operation can be manipulated in bad faith.

Practitioners in each Illinois county look to one another for trends, developments, precedents, and case results that might land on our doorstep next. Since all prosecutions are undertaken in the name of The People of the State of Illinois, and since the law-enforcement industrial complex is not limited by imaginary lines on maps, we need to know what's happening next door at all times because whatever happened "there" first is probably going to happen "here" soon. Certainly Cook County leads the way most of the time in Illinois, but the whole state criminal justice system is one giant testing lab of literal trial-and-error, and if you're ignorant of the changing tides around you, then you aren't playing the game to the best of your ability.

While Dotson grabbed the headlines in the city, the collar counties were beginning to have some of their most outrageous railroading jobs exposed by DNA as well, some of which made national news. In 1983 ten-year-old Jeanine Nicarico was murdered in DuPage County, Cook County's immediate neighbor to the west. Rolando Cruz was the lead of three co-defendants who were tried for rape and murder in that case. Cruz and Alejandro Hernandez were convicted and sentenced to death in 1985, but the third co-defendant's case resulted in a hung jury, and the State subsequently dropped the charges against him. DNA that had been collected from inside the little girl's body was stored, but the technology needed to build a useful profile from that DNA was still several years away.

DuPage County authorities built their case around a boot print and an alleged confession by Cruz. The boot print was initially tested by the local crime lab and could not be matched to the defendants. However, one of the prosecutors instructed the investigators to "keep their mouths shut" and sent the print to the Illinois State Police crime lab instead; again, no match. They ordered a third test by an independent lab in Kansas; no match. For the fourth review they sent the prints to the FBI; still no match. Despite four negative results that obviously didn't satisfy them by providing the answer they were after, they dug up an anthropologist who was the only advocate on earth of a pseudoscience that she called "wear-pattern analysis." Derided by critics and contemporaries as "Cinderella analysis" and "pure nonsense," this "expert" testified that not only did the print match one of the defendant's boots, but that she could also tell the height and race of the wearer. Eventually, the American Academy of Forensic Sciences sponsored a commission of 135 anthropologists, forensic scientists, lawyers, and legal scholars to review her cases and conclusions, and found that her identification methodology had no basis in science. Her evidence was, in their words, "complete hogwash."

As for the alleged confession, detectives claimed that Cruz told them he'd experienced a "vision" of certain aspects of the crime, and that his statement contained "details only the killer could know." That tired trope always conveniently lops off half the truth, the fact that the cops know them too. Using those details to fabricate a confession that simply never occurred, an independent commission ultimately concluded that the "dream statement" was a likely fantasy itself, and one officer admitted to having lied about reporting it. Contrary to all logic, procedure, and professionalism, the purported confession had not been reported in any contemporaneous notes or police reports, let alone written or recorded, nor was it mentioned in police testimony at the preliminary hearing, the entire point of which is to establish probable cause to charge the defendant. Proving that the framing of Cruz and Hernandez was intentional and not just a tragic error made in the zealous pursuit of justice, the investigators also suppressed the confession of the man who was ultimately proved to be the actual murderer, Brian Dugan, who told authorities of his sole responsibility for the crimes against Nicarico as part of his efforts to negotiate his way out of the death penalty in two other similar cases. Cruz and Hernandez were put on trial three times—*the third trial even after the DNA evidence was matched to Dugan*—before finally being acquitted on a directed verdict in 1995. Seven law-enforcement officials were eventually prosecuted for conspiracy to frame the defendants, but it was a hollow gesture and they were all acquitted in a sick joke of a bench trial.

Cook's neighbor to the north is Lake County, separated by the eponymous Lake Cook Road. There, in 1992, eleven-year-old Holly Staker was raped and murdered, having been strangled and stabbed dozens of times while she was babysitting two young children. Juan Rivera was in jail on a minor property charge when he came to the attention of police via a tip from an inmate who told them that Rivera was talking about knowing who killed Staker. Rivera was interviewed, but either lied or was just plain wrong about his whereabouts on the night of the crime. However, it would have been incredibly easy to establish his actual location: on the night of the crime, Rivera was wearing an electronic monitoring system device on his ankle that stemmed from a prior conviction, and EMS records showed that he hadn't left his home that night. Fingerprints taken from the crime scene did not match Rivera either, but for whatever reason, that didn't dissuade police from focusing on him.

What mattered to the police and prosecution was Rivera's "confession." During questioning that lasted several days, the man who had a history of mental illness suffered an "acute psychotic break" (as later determined by medical review), but his interrogators administered heavy psychotropic medications and pressed on. He gave several different versions of statements that the detectives characterized as admissions, but when they noticed that the details he provided did not match the facts, they simply questioned him further and goaded him into a cleaner account. One of the eventual appellate decisions in Rivera's favor pointedly noted that every piece of information that supposedly came from Rivera was wrong—except for details that had been known to the police prior to questioning. The police fed him bits of the puzzle, used leading questions to trick him into repeating them, and congratulated themselves on their sleuthing.

The "smoking gun" of fabrication was Rivera's shoes. While in jail awaiting trial, Rivera traded his shoes with another inmate who was somehow incentivized or forced to turn them over to investigators. Sure enough, testing on the shoes revealed the blood of Holly Staker, and the State eagerly disclosed their intent to introduce them at trial. They were hugely important since they were the only physical evidence that linked Rivera directly to the scene of the crime. However, defense investigators diligently proved that the shoes were not available for sale in the United States before the murder. They took things even further by showing that the exact pair in question were purchased from a Walmart *after the crime had occurred*. Confronted with the impossibility of the shoes having been at the scene of the crime, the State withdrew them as evidence. The question of how the victim's blood got onto shoes that were indisputably not at the crime scene was not immediately addressed, but at least the shoes were preserved rather than destroyed. When the shoes were ultimately retested in 2015, the blood contained two distinct genetic markers: those of Holly Staker and a still-unidentified set that is certainly not Rivera's. The shoes became ironclad proof that law-enforcement officers blatantly planted blood from the crime scene to frame their suspect. If not for the relative miracle of the shoes' timeline of availability, they might have succeeded. Rivera had been convicted three separate times and served a total of twenty years before lawyers from Stanford Law School, the prestigious firm of Jenner & Block, and the Center on Wrongful Convictions were finally able to get the Illinois Appellate Court to rule that Rivera's conviction was "unjustified and cannot stand." Not that the public defenders hadn't tried, but they lacked that extra *gravitas* that in Illinois we call "clout." Lake County prosecutors have repeatedly earned themselves a reputation for advancing patently absurd nonsense when it comes to explaining away DNA that contradicts their theory of a case. To explain the non-Rivera semen in Holly Staker's vagina, they argued she was a sexually active eleven-year-old girl who must've been with another man immediately prior to being murdered. There was not a single objective bit of evidence to support that wild claim, but it wasn't even the most outrageous hypothesis they ever advanced.

That title belongs to their theory in the case of Jerry Hobbs, charged in 2005 with the murder of his daughter Laura and her friend Krystal Tobias. The girls were eight and nine years old when they were attacked in a park near Laura's home. Both girls were stabbed repeatedly in the face and neck, and their bodies were placed next to each other in a manner that suggested ritualistic slaughter and staged posing. Jerry himself found the bodies, but unfortunately for him, he had also been recently released from prison in Texas for a violent crime that involved chasing someone with a chainsaw, so he was immediately considered the prime suspect.

Since the bodies were found fully clothed and the medical examiner did not observe signs of sexual assault, DNA swabs that had been collected as a matter of protocol went untested. A DNA sample that did not match Jerry was collected from under Krystal's fingernails, but by then the police were unwaveringly focused on building a case against Jerry. He was interrogated at length and gave a confession, the alleged motive for the killings being Laura's misbehavior in being outside when she was supposed to be grounded. When the subsequent defense investigation proved that the police forensic examiners completely missed semen in Laura's mouth, vagina, and anus, and that the DNA from those samples excluded Jerry as the source, the prosecution asserted that the girls had rolled around on the ground in the park where strangers had been fucking—apparently buck naked, and with their mouths wide open?—and that's why the evidence didn't fit their case.

The State stubbornly refused to pursue the truth. Lake County Public Defenders had to sue the FBI to force them to run the DNA results through their database of cataloged offenders. When they did, the results matched Jorge Torrez, a serial killer and former Marine who had been a friend of Krystal's older brother, and who was already imprisoned in Virginia. Jerry Hobbs was released after five years of pretrial detention that included *four years in solitary confinement*. Asked how the cops had broken him, he said: "I found my daughter's body, not them. She had no eyeballs, they'd been cut out of her skull. They didn't need to break me; I was already broken."

To complete the Chicagoland bingo card of framing innocent men for murder, the county on our southern border, Will County, produced the Fox case in 2004. Riley Fox was just a baby—only three years old—when she was abducted from her home in the middle of the night, raped, and murdered. She'd been bound with duct tape, gagged, assaulted, and drowned in a creek a few miles from her home. It took several days to find her body, enough time for media attention and speculation to build as the searches took place. Her father, Kevin Fox, had been the last adult to see her alive, so the standard law-enforcement playbook dictated that he was first on the suspect list.

By then it was common procedure to check for DNA in cases like that, and a thorough set of swabs were taken during the autopsy. However, initial results of the DNA analysis at the Illinois State Police crime lab showed "no foreign contributors" for most of the swabs and were "inconclusive" as to a check for saliva in the genitals. More detailed testing could be done at the FBI lab in Virginia, but a high volume of requests meant waiting through a backlog of approximately nine months.

Fortunately, there was another excellent clue: a pair of shoes that was found in the water near the body. The shoes should have been very easily traced by investigators because they had been purchased from an Illinois prison canteen by an inmate *who had written his name on them*. If the police had pursued that lead, they would've known that the same ex-con who left his shoes at the scene of the crime had also broken into the house next door to the Fox home on the night of the murder. Even though they didn't specifically seek that man out for questioning, we know what would have happened if they had, because he was approached by an officer during a routine canvass for witnesses during the days before the body was found, whereupon he blurted out, "Have they found that little girl yet?" and then he vomited.

Instead of focusing on the only person on earth who could be connected to both the scene of the abduction and the scene where the body was dumped, investigators inexplicably ignored the shoes and directed their attention on the last man seen with the girl, her father. He and his wife were cooperative. They sat for interviews, gave DNA samples, and consented to several searches of their home and vehicles. Nothing as significant as the shoes turned up against the father, but nothing concrete excluded him either. Days stretched into weeks, then months. The heat being generated by a combination of a horrific case, media coverage, and an impending election for state's attorney created tremendous public and political pressure for a resolution. Eight days before the election, and four days after the incumbent state's attorney's father had been arrested on federal corruption charges in Chicago, Kevin Fox was summoned to the police station for further questioning. He and his wife still believed that DNA would clear them, so they didn't hesitate to go, and they didn't bother to bring a lawyer.

The interrogation of Kevin Fox is the quintessential paragon of coercive manipulation. They began with an exhausted man who had been up since before dawn in order to work a long shift at his job. They summoned him for a nighttime interview that intentionally began after the cycle of the working day, out of circadian rhythms of rational thought. It doesn't sound like much, certainly not like anything that would be considered abuse or torture, but even that interruption in the cycle of productivity and rest takes the body and mind into a place of disorientation and distortion. If there was any doubt that was intentional, it's erased immediately to learn that he was interrogated for fourteen hours straight. No good-faith interviews, conversations, or exams of any kind last that long, over those hours, or under those conditions, especially not those that demand complete precision for the sake of accuracy, like a reliable investigation in a major criminal case. Locked in a typical "interview room" that is, in reality, a sensory-deprivation chamber, the subject is quickly overwhelmed by isolation and fear. The fuel thrown on that fire is the highest possible quotient of emotional distress. The topic of discussion was nothing less than the abduction, rape, and murder of Fox's own toddler daughter. They showed him pictures of her body—limp, cold, victimized, bruised, and dirtied—discarded in the water like someone's trash. On top of those emotions, they added a layer of their power at its essence, confronting him with no less authority than the absolute certainty of law enforcement. They lied about the strength of their "evidence" in the form of an allegedly failed lie-detector test that is so unreliable, it's regarded as a pseudoscience that isn't admissible in any US court. Still, they presented it as irrefutable proof of his guilt. They combined his pain with simple, almost clichéd psychological manipulation in the form of the old good cop/bad cop routine, wherein one officer demonstrates fury and a barely contained appetite for revenge, while another offers the lifeboat of comfort, sympathy, and understanding. One cop screams about the death penalty while the second postulates that the crime was an accident that can be explained and forgiven with the proper contrition. Exhaustion, pain, anger, and false hope in the face of utter hopelessness: that is the recipe to break a man. The authorities wanted a resolution, a headline arrest in the biggest case of their careers, a reason to win the election, and a restored sense of calm for an entire community. Kevin Fox just gave them what they wanted. He spent "only" eight months in jail as an accused child killer before thorough DNA testing led investigators back to the man who'd written his name on the shoes he left behind with the body of his victim.

I knew about Dotson, Cruz, and Rivera when I went for the interview to become a prosecutor. I also knew about the daily realities of prosecuting drug cases, and the possibility that I would be required at some point to argue in favor of the death penalty, another area where DNA was exposing Illinois's shameful past just as quickly as technology and politics allowed. About the only thing I had going for me was the fact that I really wanted to lend my strengths to public service. I love Chicago, and I hate the violence, I hate the suffering; I've experienced loss, and our tragedies make me sad and angry. Probably most defense attorneys would love to be prosecutors, to prevent the abuse of power from the side that has a real chance to rein it in. If there was a way to guarantee we could be anti-corruption crusaders and investigators of violent crimes—without the absurd cruelties of the drug laws and the obsequious deference to petty tyrants who see themselves as so special that they have the nerve to consider themselves a separate race with slogans like Blue Lives Matter—we'd sign up in an instant. Systemic injustices absolutely lit a fire in me.

Unfortunately, I blew the interview by asking if I would be allowed to dismiss cases where I thought the cops were lying. A famous rule of wielding power is that politics is the art of compromise, and I guess I just wasn't ready to make certain sacrifices.

Before the Public Defender's Office created the Forensic Science Division and took DNA cases away from Felony Trial grunts like me, I had one case where genetic samples were alleged to supplement the other scientific evidence against my client. The case was a bit of a heater because it centered around the stolen Heisman Trophy ring of Notre Dame football legend Johnny Lattner. Police alleged that there was an argument among several of the guys in the crew who'd committed the theft about how to move the merch and maximize profit from it, and that argument led to a triple shooting in Evanston that was pinned on my client. He had been at the scene and was tested for gunshot residue, or GSR, the amount of which can strongly imply if a person discharged a firearm, was in very close proximity to such a discharge, handled a recently fired weapon, or was just close enough to catch traces of the cloud of telltale chemicals.

The weird part was that there seemed to be more evidence of my client's innocence than there was of his guilt: the GSR levels were trace amounts only and were found on the backs of his hands, indicating that he had not been the shooter but had rather put his hands up in a defensive position in response to being threatened. My client's statement to the cops was almost verbatim "Fuck you, I didn't do shit." He had a rock-solid alibi for the theft itself, and most importantly, there were multiple witnesses who'd alleged that the shooter was someone else entirely. When I asked him why he thought he was being charged, he explained that the lead detective had a personal grudge against him stemming from his youthful background of being kind of a knucklehead from a family whose name was well-known to the Evanston Police Department. That seemed fair enough because his family was indeed notorious, and the lead detective was a woman who was widely reputed among our Evanston clients to be a vengeful narcissist with little regard for the truth and an insatiable taste for power.

Defendants tend to give PDs nicknames; if you're a young white guy with glasses and a decent reputation for winning some cases, they call you Clark Kent or Superman (which they pronounce "Supa-man"). The ones who are prejudiced against white people call you Joe, to emphasize that all white people are the same to them. Early on in this case, my client came to me and said that his family had scraped together enough money for one of two things: he could either bond himself out, or he could hire a private attorney—but not both. He was adamant that he was innocent, so he said, "Supaman, I need to know if you got this or if I need to go private." I told him to put it down on his freedom and expressed it in proper street terminology by just saying "bet." We talked about the fact that the State was promising to reveal evidence of my client's DNA on the gun, but he was sure they were lying and I was confident that even if they weren't, I could argue that the GSR contradicted the allegation that he'd been the shooter, so his DNA on the weapon only proved that he'd handled it, not that he'd pulled the trigger. Plus we had the witnesses who'd fingered someone else entirely, so I was really confident. The prosecutor was one of the most feared in the local branch, whose husband had been something of a hero in the FBI's Operation Greylord, which exposed corruption in Cook County courts, and I was really excited to take her on because I felt I had a somewhat rare winner. They dragged the case out for months, taking continuances under the reasoning of needing more time to get the results of the DNA testing. My client was pissed about being on bond for so long and wanted to demand a speedy trial, but with him out instead of in, I counseled that we could afford to be patient instead of risking any knockout surprises.

On the day that the trial was finally supposed to go forward, after several warnings from the judge that he wouldn't tolerate any additional delays, I was standing in the hallway with my client when the prosecutor snuck into the courtroom without us, had the case called, and dropped it without any explanation whatsoever. The legal terminology is *nolle prosequi*, an obscure Latin phrase that the ASAs pronounce as "nolly pros," like if you just cut off the word "process" in the middle, without the "ess." She turned tail and ran before we even got inside to hear the words. On the one hand, it was disappointing to know that someone whom I'd professionally admired had participated in a dishonest scheme to keep my client in jeopardy by being subject to conditions of bond that made him arrestable without proper constitutional protections like probable cause; plus, he also lost 10 percent of his money to the institutional graft of "Court Clerk processing fees," and that was a big chunk of change. On the other hand, a win is a win, and this one was big. "You were right, Supaman, thank you" were words I never got tired of hearing.

To the very end of my government days, I had a fantasy of asking to be allowed to help investigate my friend David Chereck's case, but I was too afraid to get caught up in some reflexive protocol that might make them suspicious of me just for asking. Thankfully, DNA eventually resulted in the capture and conviction of his killer. In my mind's eyes and ears, I can still see David's face and goofy haircut, hear his voice, and remember bits of our conversations. I sometimes wonder what he would have become. Statistically, probably not the attorney general of the United States, but someone's husband, someone's father, and, based on his sense of humor and joy, probably the light of someone's life. I have to imagine what Jeanine Nicarico was like, but it isn't difficult. She was almost exactly my age. She lived in the suburbs of Chicago, just as I did. She had a family and a lifestyle I could quite easily understand. On the day of her murder, she'd stayed home from school sick, hanging out in her pajamas and watching TV, just like every other kid I ever knew. Her mom had come home from work to feed her lunch, and they got to experience the fleeting mercy of a final hug and kiss. The savage barbarian who ended her life and took much of the joy of living from her family had kicked in the door, bound her body with a sheet, taped a towel around her head, raped her vaginally and anally, smashed her skull to pieces as he bludgeoned her to death, and dumped her corpse in a field. Her demise was the very definition of brutality and cruelty. When her sisters were married in the decades after the crime, on each occasion the bridal group went straight from the ceremony to the cemetery, placing the bouquet that would have been Jeanine's bridesmaid's flowers on her gravestone instead. Her family, and so many others, live with ghosts, questions, and fantasies of lives unlived. Defense attorneys are filled with the same rage toward child killers that the police and prosecutors feel—not the same pain as the victims' parents, but a deep human sympathy for their suffering, nonetheless. Not many people are able or inclined to empathize with the people who face false accusations, wear the shackles, are dragged before the cameras to be thrown in cages of cinder block and steel, and have their precious time on planet earth irreplaceably stolen from them by crazed tyrants. To those of us at the defense table, sometimes the victimization feels almost the same.

VI. PLEA DEALS

Public defenders do not get the very best plea deals; we get standardized offers from the State that are worked out by an unwritten formula. Reviews for an offer start with the crime itself, and the sentencing range assigned by the law for the main count or counts. The first practical question is "Was anybody hurt, and if so, how badly?" If it's a property crime like a theft, they will do the math on the damages or losses. Those punishments will be worse if the stealing occurred in the context of a relationship that was exploited, such as employee or caretaker. Then you follow a relatively simple script regarding history: What is the defendant's background? Any priors? If it's a first offense, the defendant probably gets the minimum. If not, the sentence for the new case has to be higher than the last one.

The prosecutorial mindset in plea negotiations was laid out for me by several colleagues in the defense bar who had been federal prosecutors before leaving the government to become private defense attorneys. They explained to me that the key approach when seeking a deal is one of these two: either you have a genuinely strong defense that truly threatens the government with losing the case, or the defendant is facing a punishment that he or she genuinely does not deserve. Those former prosecutors who become defense counselors market themselves to prospective clients by claiming that their expertise in building cases gives them unique insight into defeating them as well. Maybe their experience helps, but I find defending cases to be a specific mindset and skill that improves with experience and is fundamentally based on a particular philosophical orientation. I think prosecutorial bosses implicitly agree with me, because defense attorneys can almost never become prosecutors due to a law-enforcement ethos that demands loyalty to "the team" to the point of near-total disregard of any merit in defending people or their rights. At least PDs can become judges, although only very few do.

The turncoat hired guns are actually relying on their connections to make better plea deals for the inflated fees that justify them leaving government work behind. That is the special benefit they provide, and they do it quite well, since cases can have a huge range of possible outcomes where the goal is a mutually beneficial resolution. If the best plan is to beg for mercy, that approach carries more weight to prosecutors coming from one of their own. If a strong defense is an option, committed defense attorneys will usually push their client to go to trial (whether or not the person whose liberty is on the line can be persuaded is another question). Real leverage comes from presenting a credible threat of a potential loss to seek the guaranteed benefits of significantly reduced charges or punishment. Either way, you have to make your pitch directly to a boss; courtroom ASAs will not have the authority to give you the best deals, and they won't make your case to their supervisors as well as you can.

Given the sheer volume of criminal cases in a city like Chicago, charges become routine, and sentencing does too. For example, simple drug possession usually gets you "drug school" the first time so that you can keep your permanent record clean. Second offenses get second chances—probation that can also be cleaned off your record if you complete drug treatment successfully. Then real probation and a permanent conviction on your third. A fourth could bring time, but there is a way to avoid it with intense probation or maybe boot camp, especially if the jails are particularly overcrowded. From then on, it's the pen.

Many people who've gotten that far actually prefer prison to paper since they don't have to deal with a probation officer or a ridiculous avalanche of probation fees, and a year sentence after credits for good behavior works out to six months or less, whereas probation can be a constant albatross around their necks for two or three years. Time credits can be complicated since they aren't guaranteed and can be awarded or denied seemingly at the whim of corrections officers and circumstances beyond any rational control or prediction. However, there has been a long-standing pattern in Illinois of people sentenced to a year in prison actually serving only sixty-one days. To explain this, there was a rumor about obscure accounting bureaucracy. Apparently, state government budgetary months were rounded to thirty days. Once a prisoner was in for any amount of time longer than two months, the Illinois Department of Corrections (or maybe the specific institution) was eligible to, and in fact did, receive funds from the State to feed and house that person for a whole year. Therefore, the hustle by IDOC was to get as many nonviolent inmates as possible who were sentenced to one-year terms (primarily low-level drug possession convicts), kick them out on the sixty-first day, and take the money and run. It was so common that defense attorneys, prosecutors, and judges all over the state routinely stretched ethical boundaries to dangle that number to defendants as a plea incentive. Defendants all knew about it too, and many came prepared to plea discussions seeking their sixty-one days. It beats the shit out of dealing with probation.

Prosecutors serve assignment rotations between various trial divisions, and one rotation is called Felony Review, where their principal responsibility is to determine the preliminary charges to file in a given case. Many cases are straightforward and routine, but in more complex or serious cases such as felony violence or premeditated property crimes, they utilize a practice of maximizing negotiating leverage by either horizontal or vertical overcharging. Horizontal overcharging is the practice of filing an expanded set of charges of the same severity on the same set of facts. The extra counts are typically based on different subchapters of the same law. For example, possession of a weapon can be upgraded or charged as possession of a weapon on a public way; possession within certain distance of a school, a church or other house of worship, or a playground; possession by a felon, or while being a gang member, or while associating with known felons or gang members; possession of an unlicensed weapon or one with a defaced serial number; possession while loaded, uncased, or immediately accessible in a vehicle, and other permutations.

Vertical overcharging is simply adding more serious counts despite the facts not really justifying extremely severe punishment, knowing that the higher charge(s) can be easily dropped as part of a plea to a lesser. That way the defendant feels like they're getting a huge benefit, even though the government never really intended to proceed or to win on the most serious count. This is most often seen in cases with multiple defendants, where the government wants leverage over one of them in order to improve their strategic position against another one, called a "co-defendant," or just "co-d."

For me, the more plea negotiations I experienced, the more I got a feeling of them being a sort of game, and that started to corrode my notions of justice very deeply. Knowing that vagaries of personality, mood, career ambition, persistence, and connections (among many others) can produce vastly different outcomes for defendants with nearly identical sets of facts—or even detrimental outcomes for people with significantly better facts in their favor—gives the entire field of criminal law an artifice that incentivizes "winning" and practicality over ethics. It always bothered me that prosecutors never give a felony offer in terms of time lesser than years. It was always years. They round up or down to years, like all the time in a person's life that flows between has no value or meaning to them. I tried once to do the conversion for them as a percentage of life expectancy of an American minority living below the poverty line in public housing; they got incredibly pissed about how irrelevant they thought that was. I also snapped once at a prosecutor who was being stubborn about a transactional plea on a property offense because I thought she was being too formulaic about background instead of taking any time to consider the impact of a three-year prison sentence instead of two years. I asked her sarcastically to explain what difference it would make to her personally and added a smear like "It's not like you give a shit." That's a mistake I wish I hadn't made, but I tell myself that it's the sort of thing you get out of your system while you're young.

Many of the persons handing out the sentences do care: they want the convict to suffer. A common prosecutorial mentality that I observed was that the criminal deserves punishment. There is no way to measure what it feels like to be incarcerated until you get a taste of it for yourself, but that's impossible to quantify in the gamesmanship of the administration of justice. It's such cruel irony that the essence of sociopathy is lack of empathy for others, and that to be a prosecutor or judge, one of the essential criteria is that you must not have experienced the exact punishment you seek to impose on others.

My taste of incarceration came professionally. I was conducting a client visit in one of the maximum-security divisions at the Cook County Jail, Division 11, which at that time did not have one specific place for attorney visits. The deputies had to bring you onto the actual tier to meet your client. After passing through standard screening, the sheriffs would bring you to an office to wait for an escort to the deck where your client was being held. That division had a wheel-and-spoke layout, so after an elevator ride to whatever floor, you'd walk down a long hallway to the heavy steel sally-port doors that were gateways to the outer rings of the cellblocks. Just inside the entry was another long hallway; on one side was an indoor recreation room with a few basketball hoops. On the other side were one or two small meeting rooms that were usually for classes or counseling meetings, and those were used for the privacy of attorney-client conferences. About ninety feet down the hallway from the entrance was an elevated security desk, from which the deputies could see the sally port, the rec room, the cellblocks, and the doors to the meeting rooms.

Each meeting room was the same on every floor: cinder-block, monochrome-white chambers with a thick glass window to the hallway, and the bare essentials of furniture in the form of tiny steel tables and welded steel stools. Lit only by fluorescent light and stinking like cigarettes, the doors were heavy solid steel, and there was an intercom with a button to call the security desk. The sheriffs would point you into the room and go off to get your client while you waited, which could take anywhere from five minutes to an hour depending on whether he was "home" or not. Once they brought him to the room, you'd be locked in there together and had to buzz up to the watch desk to be released. If the buzzer wasn't working, which it usually wasn't, you just had to pound on the glass until somebody heard you. Using a pen works best, since the click of the plastic against the glass stands out a little better above the din, and it hurts your hand less than using your wedding ring or bare knuckles.

That particular visit went well. I had new reports and pictures to show my client as we prepared for his trial. He was pleased that I was making progress, that we had a strategy, and with just being visited. When we finished, I alerted the tower and they buzzed us out into the hallway. We closed the door behind us as instructed to wait for our escorts. The deputies shouted for him to walk back up to the tier and told me to wait a minute so they could call someone from the main desk to bring me back outside.

Standing in the hallway waiting, I heard the distinct electric buzzer of another gate being opened, followed by a loud metallic click. It was rec time for one of the tiers, and I was standing at the entrance to the basketball court when the final barrier between me and an entire deck of maximum-security inmates was unlocked. I was standing there alone, a young white guy in civilian clothes, cornered against two locked doors and cinder-block walls, with dozens of inmates coming straight toward me and no deputies in sight. I remembered a lesson that one of my friends in the sheriff's office told me about his training in the police academy for situations where an officer finds himself without his partner, badge, gun, or radio: Even without any tools or any backup, *"You always have your authority."* I had the confidence of my office, and some comfort from the cameras, but I could see that the desk was unattended while head counts were being done or whatever other issues take the attention of guards who are moving masses of detainees.

It's just human nature that if you've been cooped up for a while, getting out of that monotony produces a burst of energy and appetite for new stimulus. Fortunately, most of the inmates didn't care about anything but the basketball court and the rec room. There were so many of them that the ones in the back of the pack couldn't even see that I was there. But some immediately started jeering with excitement and encircling me as soon as they laid eyes on me. I was scanning for familiar faces as fast as possible, trying to find anyone I was representing who might recognize the value in preserving mutual respect and my health, but none were to be found.

It took the deputies almost forty-five minutes to remember I was there and to come and get me. Not even one full hour, let alone a day, or a week, or a month, or a year. None of the inmates were physically rough with me, unless you count the physical proximity of their intimidation. What I endured was a steady stream of verbal jousting with a select group of dangerous people in a pack dynamic and a highly volatile environment. They enjoyed my discomfort. Some of their baiting was seethingly racial; some was virulently anti-government. My strategy was to maintain my composure by asking about their cases, their PDs, their judges, and sympathizing as much as possible with their plights and offering tokens of advice. I occasionally mentioned that the intercom was on and that the cameras could bring the SORT officers (the Special Operations Response Team—the deputies the inmates truly feared), but none of us knew if that was true or not.

A few seemed to have endless energy to engage. It felt like forever. I was absolutely terrified.

Not too many prosecutors, judges, or cops will ever know what it feels like to be cornered by a mob of inmates. Thankfully I still have no idea what it's like to be actually incarcerated for any extended period of time, left to the dangers in the corners and blind spots of a maximum-security jail. But for whoever has to endure it, whether there is moral justification for their incarceration or not, just know that every single moment in a lockup is spent on razor's edge, fraught with danger and stress that puts the struggle for physical and emotional survival front and center with little room for anything else except that overwhelming desperation to get out. The pressure changes everyone, breaking them down, creating something entirely different where the prior version of themselves had been.

That's why it's so appalling to hear years tossed around like candy, especially for drug and property crimes where nobody got hurt. I've gotten offers for sentences of days, but only after the fact; it's called "time considered served," or TCS for short. Prosecutors make that offer when it's more expedient to resolve a case than to stretch it out. Eventually the courts created a second, parallel designation of "time actually served" to clarify the record. It was really done to prevent political criticism, but at least it had the unintended benefit of lessening the insult on a person's experience. But I've never gotten, or even heard of, an offer for something like four months, twelve days, and six hours. That kind of math just does not exist in courtrooms. Round numbers make the assembly line go faster, and the human cost has almost no place in the equation.

There are some offers that surprise even the most experienced attorneys, when they are far enough outside the norm. We had a client with a rap sheet as long as possible for someone his age. He was a homeless man with a panoply of "minor" mental illnesses and a severe drug problem. He was a prime example of the vastly different ways that prosecutors and defense attorneys see people:

To prosecutors, he was the personification of irredeemable recidivism, only worthy of being kept locked up for as long as possible on each charge so that society would be spared any more of his selfish damages; to us, he was a desperately lost soul, generally harmless despite the rash of property crimes and drug cases that formed his life's work. I honestly have no idea exactly how many priors he had because there were too many to count. Records of a person's arrest and conviction history were kept by the Illinois State Police Bureau of Identification, so they were sometimes referred to as someone's "B of I." I could almost tell by the way they walked that the ASAs had a whopper on their hands and were about to serve me a B of I that looked more like a small-town phone book than an individual's criminal history report. This guy's was massive, the kind of epic criminal curriculum vitae that would make experienced practitioners stop what they were doing and just read it for a while, then bring it back to the office to pass around over the lunch table while checking to see whether anyone there had represented him before and, if so, share those memories too.

B of I's include each person's unique fingerprint identification number as assigned by the FBI, and that is the main way that authorities from different jurisdictions can be sure that a single person is the same individual across places and time. That is also why giving an alias is pretty useless, despite the wonderful creativity some people exhibit in response to the somewhat sensitive question of "What is your name?" In addition to arrests and convictions, a person's background (aka history, rap sheet, or jacket) also lists any occasions that police or courts took action to address suspected mental illness and the outcome of that process.

Whenever there is the chance that a defendant has a mental illness or disorder that could be preventing them from understanding the process they're in, or the punishments they could be facing, or from being able to participate in presenting their defense by speaking with or listening to their lawyers, we were ethically obligated to send them for a mental exam at the jail. It's called a "behavioral clinical examination," or BCX. There are staff doctors who specialize in the diagnosis and treatment of various mental conditions, although the treatments are usually just a fistful of pills that the defendant may or may not be willing to take. For court purposes, BCX reports tell the judge and the lawyers if, in the opinion of the expert doctors at the jail, the defendant is fit for trial; only fit if he or she is taking medication ("fit with meds"); unfit for trial (which may be temporary); has a specific diagnosis that may form the basis of either a defense or mitigation of diminished capacity; or, in very rare cases, is insane. In the Public Defender's Office, many of us got the feeling that the bar for the findings to come back as unfit, verifiably ill, or insane was way out of touch with the realities we were experiencing in our interactions with the defendants, but we were neither medical experts nor objective.

Defendants generally hated being sent for a BCX because it meant additional delays in resolving their cases, and if you've ever dealt with anyone who genuinely has a mental illness or disorder, then you know they are often in angry denial about it and resent the implications. Once a defendant gets sent for a BCX at any point along his or her criminal career, it's very likely that they will be sent again each time they have a new case. Whatever considerations the police use in deciding whether someone needs a mental exam, there is a whole set of considerations to take into account between a lawyer and client when we are deciding whether or not to order such an evaluation. Our determinations are mostly based on time spent together talking and the feelings we get about their lucidity or capacity, things that some lawyers are more sensitive to than others. Unfortunately, when I was there, we got very minimal formal training in detecting symptoms of mental problems, which amounted to "you'll know if something feels off, and then you better CYA." Although most of the inmates hate the mental exam process, a few know it's coming and relish the chance to get out of general population, if only for a few hours or a few days. Sometimes if a defendant is being too aggressive to the point that even his or her own lawyer is fed up, a BCX can be ordered just to remind them that we have some control over their fates and they better remember and respect that. In any event, the decision is easiest when we know the person has been down that road before, another one of the many ways that precedents matter in various contexts of practicing law.

Among many other red flags we might use for making the decision to order a BCX is hygiene. Even though we are very accustomed to meeting people with different standards and abilities to maintain themselves, and even though the jail is supposed to be providing basic health care for the detainees too, sometimes you experience something new. The defendant with the Dickensian rap sheet not only had prior BCXs all over his history, but he also had dreadlocks down to his knees that had become infested with gnats at some point either before or during his pretrial detention. He also had open sores on various parts of his body and was dealing with complications from untreated diabetes. Every medical issue we identified was referred through the proper channels, and we were hoping the combination of his physical state and the results of a new BCX would confirm our suspicions and serve as sufficient basis to persuade the judge to divert him out of prison and into treatment.

The State was having none of it. As decent as they could be on a human level when the stenographer was gone, on the record I never saw a single prosecutor swerve away from punishment as the only appropriate response to misbehavior. Based on his record, despite the fact that he only had a drug possession case, the ASAs wanted at least six years. I can't say we were horrified, considering his sheet. Unsurprisingly, when we conveyed that offer to the man himself, he declined. Actually—and this was more surprising than his rejection of the offer—he literally flung shit at the PD who presented it. That episode earned him special treatment from the sheriffs; when they felt it necessary, they could put people in straitjackets and other unconventional restraints, one of which included a motorcycle helmet that they usually reserved for spitters. Once the feces flew, they decided not to take any chances with him going forward, and they brought him off the elevator looking like a combination of Hannibal Lecter and a member of Parliament-Funkadelic.

Having arrived at an impasse where his latest exam officially deemed him fit for trial, he had no defense, he would not plead, nobody at the courthouse actually thought he could sit through a trial, and everybody just wanted the whole thing to end, we sent a small team of PDs into an off-the-record plea conference with a judge who had just been promoted to the Felony Trial Division and was taking over the call of a recently retired veteran. I'm sure the new judge wasn't too thrilled to have this whole mess land on him, but it seemed to provide us with an opportunity. At the time, a new type of intensive drug probation was being offered by the TASC drug-treatment program that had special authorization to work with Cook County in an official, court-sanctioned capacity. Reading the language of the TASC probation rules, it was clearly intended to be a measure of last resort that was reserved for the most desperate of addicts. Although severe mental illness was supposed to prevent admittance to the program, we were able to convince the TASC counselor to conditionally accept our client if the judge would go along.

After a disproportionately intense plea conference that featured two teams of lawyers going back and forth over what was really kind of a minor case, the judge said he would give our client probation. One of the ASAs actually screamed and ran to get their bosses, presumably so that they could go together to tell the chief judge what a travesty this new judge was being. We decided not to wait until the ink was dry on the offer and ran to the lockup to deliver the good news that we were sure would end this whole frustrating saga, but as mental illness often does, it prevented our client from realizing the value of his opportunity and he refused the deal. Now we were the ones who were shouting and running for our bosses. Either sensing the opportunity to avoid a bad reputation with the State, or having been explicitly instructed to do so, the judge used the defendant's rejection of miraculous release as the basis to order yet another BCX. When he passed that one and continued to persist with his intransigence, he was eventually forced to go to trial, whereupon he got dunked and took twelve the hard way.

He had freedom at his fingertips—all he had to do was sign—but he ended up dying in prison instead. We never got a TASC offer again for anyone with more than four or five priors; he totally shut down that option for everyone who came after him.

Plea deals usually stay the course of general predictability, but sometimes the initial offer is so bad that the defense only begins to investigate the less-obvious defenses after getting it, trying to find some leverage that will make enough of an impression on the State for them to reconsider. One of my first major heaters was a case involving a man charged with home invasion and forcible rape. The details of the crime were horrible, but in and of themselves would not have made the case an outlier. What changed things in a tangible way were the recordings of the two 911 calls that were made from inside the house. One was from the main victim herself, who'd heard the defendant break in through her kitchen window and called the police. Despite being confronted by the defendant while she was on the phone, she'd managed to hide her cordless from his view and had the presence of mind to keep the line open while he raped her on her bed. The second call was from her young daughter, who'd heard her mother's screams as everything was unfolding and took another phone with her as she hid under her bed. Her abject terror came through quite clearly, not only the first time you heard the recording, but every single loop after that as well. Owing to the defendant's status as a decorated veteran of the first Iraq War, the State very generously offered him twenty-three years on a plea.

With nothing to lose and nobody else particularly eager to help,

I accepted the chance to explore the defendant's claims that he was suffering from Gulf War Syndrome, a particularly poorly defined allegation that exposure to chemical weapons in Iraq made him lose control of his behavior. Combined with an actual diagnosis of PTSD, we were trying to shape some sort of diminished capacity defense. The Public Defender's Office granted our investigative requests for extra funds to contact various expert witnesses who were supporting the then-officially rejected proposition that Gulf War Syndrome even existed. Bolstering our chances was the fact that the defendant's job in the army had been as part of a unit whose duties were to respond to incidents of suspected use of chemical weapons, giving him uniquely high exposure to both the gases themselves and the equipment and substances that were used in response.

In all honesty, we could not find reliable evidence that Gulf War Syndrome existed, nor that there could be any provable connection between such an illness and any behavioral disorders, let alone that the defendant had GWS and that it drove his actions to the point where he could be considered less culpable, or even not guilty. What we were able to do was to produce a good quantity of military records proving aspects of his service, and a frankly disjointed set of reports from pharmacologists and psychologists about PTSD and possible reactions to chemical exposure. When the State decided all of that was worth a discount to twenty, we took it. My colleagues congratulated me on that small measure of victory, but looking back on the experience, it sure felt like everyone lost.

The holy grail of plea deals is to keep any conviction off your client's record, dropping the charges in exchange for something non-judicial like an apology, restitution, classes, or some offsetting charity. If that's out of reach, the next best thing is to avoid a felony conviction by getting those charges reduced to a misdemeanor.

For many years illegal gun possession in Illinois was a misdemeanor, owing in part to the constitutional status of the right to bear arms in America. As gun crimes began to escalate and garner more national media and political attention, new felony enhancements were created. When those didn't end the violence plaguing the streets of Chicago, a new strategy was devised to address the trend: an unwritten policy in the State's Attorney's Office to forbid plea deals that allowed the use of older sections of the weapons laws to reduce felonies to misdemeanors, as had been allowed in some cases where either the facts or the person were judged worthy of discretionary mercy. How that discretionary mercy is or isn't applied is the mystery behind the curtain.

Acknowledging that there are lawful ways to possess and use weapons, criminal charges for gun possession in Chicago are labeled as "unlawful use of a weapon," or UUWs for short. Just after the unwritten policy took effect, I had a UUW client who was a twenty-year-old black kid from the Southwest Side of the city. He'd never been in trouble before and was not in a gang; each of those points was somewhat remarkable for members of his demographic. He had a grandmother who lived more than an hour's ride away on the CTA, in one of the North Side areas that fed cases to the Skokie courthouse. She was very ill and had a doctor's appointment early one morning that she could not get to by herself, so the night before the appointment my client took the bus to her house in order to spend the night and help her the next day.

Grandma lived in a truly gang-infested neighborhood. When the kid got off the bus, he was immediately confronted by a small group of bangers who were demanding to know his affiliation—"*Rep yo set!*"—so they could decide whether to attack him or grant safe passage. It was about four blocks from the bus stop to his grandmother's house—only half a mile—and although he tried to ignore them at first, and then denied any gang ties when that didn't work, they didn't let him go. They followed him, shouting slogans and threats. When they decided he was a legitimate target, they literally ganged up on him.

One of them had a pit bull, so the transition from harassment to chase began with unleashing the beast. Several witnesses saw what was happening and called the cops, but there was no way the police were going to get there faster than a sprinting dog. The animal quickly closed ground and clenched onto the kid's arm, dragging him to the ground, kicking and screaming in pain. A desperate struggle followed, with my client being bitten on the arm, hand, and side near his hip. He managed to shake the dog off himself before the guys running behind could catch up. He got up and stumbled forward, dodging between parked cars and signposts while leaving a trail of blood in a ferocious hunt as he thrashed and sprinted to get away.

They chased him up the stoop to his grandma's house, nearly tripping up the concrete stairs, and he barreled through the door. Grandma knew the dangers of the area, and she kept a small revolver in the front-hall closet. Since they knew where he lived and could come back with reinforcements at any time, he felt the need for his own show of force; he grabbed the gun and went back outside, intending to shoot the dog. Approaching sirens convinced the chasers to grab the animal and begin to retreat, but the kid waved the pistol up where they could see it while shouting a few choice warnings of his own. Wouldn't you know it, that was the moment the blue-and-whites rolled up.

We had the 911 tapes and several witness statements about the gang chase, the medical reports from the treatment of his bites, his grandma's legal gun registration and her own medical reports to corroborate the reason for his visit, a report from the gang crime unit in that police district that verified a pattern of similar attacks in that area, and a young kid with a clean record. We knew we had a problem with the fact that he went back outside with a gun he wasn't licensed to carry instead of just closing and locking the door behind him and waiting for the police, so we weren't going to get anywhere asking for the case to be tossed entirely. I begged for the mercy of a misdemeanor instead of a felony. The State flatly refused.

With the confidence that the usual trial tax was less of a risk given the facts, and thinking that even if we lost, the chances were excellent that my client would get probation instead of prison (since it was his first offense and there were unusually strong mitigating circumstances), I gave up on plea negotiations and set the case for a bench trial. Both sides are obligated to tell the other what they intend to argue in a trial; the State does so with the charges, and the defense responds with a formal filing called an "Answer." Since we had to concede his possession of the gun, I filed my answer with a laundry list of every possibly applicable affirmative defense in the book: defense of person, defense of dwelling, defense of real or personal property, necessity, compulsion . . . basically everything except insanity. I was guided by the generally reliable rule of thumb to take winners to a bench and take losers to a jury.

That time I was wrong.

As impressed by our thorough arguments and clearly sympathetic as the judge was, he rationally dissected each of our claims and rejected them one by one, primarily relying on the simple fact that the kid could've stayed inside. At least we got to see the look of delight on the faces of the ASAs turn to outrage as the judge imposed a sentence of a single day of probation, waiving all reporting requirements and fees. But they got their pound of flesh in the form of another young black man with a felony conviction that will follow him around for the rest of his life, all for an undeniably defensive act of protecting himself and his grandmother that occurred under a set of circumstances that is totally foreign in the leafy environs of the north suburban courthouse where the case was heard.

As fate would have it, almost immediately after that case was over, and while the sting and puzzlement of it was fresh in both my mind and that of the judge, another gun possession case was assigned to our courtroom—although this one did not require the services of the public defender. A famous football player for the Chicago Bears named Tank Johnson caught a UUW of his own. Since he wasn't a

PD client, I never saw the official police reports, but the courthouse rumor was that he was out for a night of clubbing in the downtown Gold Coast area and utilized the services of a valet to park his car. The valet spotted a gun under the driver's seat and called the cops, who were very widely rumored to be so incentivized by gun arrests that they would be willing to exchange discreet favors for anyone facilitating their efforts to take a burner off the streets.

Tank was an important enough part of the Bears' march to the Super Bowl that in a scene that would probably not be repeated in the modern NFL, head coach Lovie Smith and superstar player Brian Urlacher came with him to some court appearances to walk the phalanx of cameras and journalists at the entrance. It was a show of public support that also included at least one meeting with the prosecution (and with a lot of cops in the State's Attorney's Office to sign some autographs and take some pictures) to put in a good word and some star power in the effort to spare Mr. Johnson a felony conviction that would probably derail his athletic career. Since judges have no authority to control charges being filed or withdrawn by the State, there was nothing to be done from the bench when a private deal was reached for a reduction of Tank Johnson's charges from felony to misdemeanor, even when it was done for a celebrity against the unwritten so-called policy that the State had made such a big deal out of when publicly touting their stiff stance against gun crimes in Chicago.

However, there was something the judge could do when it came time for the hearing to take Tank's plea and impose a sentence. He spoke to the prosecutors first, laying public shame to the hypocrisy of their claims of an across-the-board approach that was actually disregarded in certain backroom deals. Their selective capitulation turned their tough-on-crime slogans into more of a PR campaign than an actual law-enforcement tactic, and he made them eat that on the record.

What happened next was personally very gratifying, and I wish the kid had been there to see it for himself: Judge Epstein told the story of my twenty-year-old client to Mr. Terry "Tank" Johnson, who had a background and experiences that could make him really understand gangs and violence, and the herculean efforts it takes to pull oneself out of such an environment to become any sort of success, let alone achieve the regal perquisites of a professional athlete in America. The judge described the circumstances that saw my client running for his life, the injuries he sustained, and the terror he felt during those moments when he was completely unsure if he would make it to safety or suffer an excruciating death by teeth, fists, or bullets. He detailed our efforts to negotiate a plea, and the defenses we presented, only to be rebuffed by the State and ensnared by their aggressive application of the law. And he made the millionaire athlete say it out loud, asking him, "Who deserves the break that you are getting here today, Mr. Johnson? Who deserves it more: you or him?" The NFL star replied meekly, "He does." "That's right. And yet you're the one getting it. I hope you make the most of this chance, sir."

At least in part by virtue of that plea, Tank Johnson went on to play in the Super Bowl for the Bears, but not before he was arrested again on numerous weapons possession charges in Lake County, just north of Chicago. Johnson's friend and housemate tried to take the blame for the numerous guns and drugs found in a search of Johnson's house, but just two days after that search and arrest, Johnson and his friend went to a club downtown where the friend was shot to death. Johnson's sentence for the violation of probation was 120 days in jail, after half of which with good behavior he was discharged, TCS.

VII. CHIRAQ

My very first case was a gun case. It wasn't a shooting; it was a possession with three upgrades: the gun was loaded, and it was possessed "upon a public way" by a member of a street gang. I was just an intern with "licensed student practitioner" status, not even a fully licensed lawyer or full-time PD, but I was allowed to present cases under the supervision of experienced attorneys due to Illinois Supreme Court Rule 711, which permitted students to assist in public-interest roles (mostly governmental agencies like the offices of the State's Attorney, Attorney General, and Public Defender).

The idea of these Rule 711 internships was to gain invaluable experience while reducing the workloads of public employees, and it served as a great pipeline into these jobs after graduation. In my case, the pipeline was so direct that when I was eventually hired two years later, I got my first felony assignment to the very same courtroom where I interned. The cases in that courtroom were all from Chicago—the city itself, not the suburbs—and mostly from the North Side of the city that included the housing projects of Cabrini-Green and the Lathrop Homes. All the cases carried the threat of penitentiary sentences, but many allowed for the possibility of probation, or even lesser punishments like a dismissal or conditional release that could be earned by successful completion of treatment or classes. The stakes were high, there was an endless supply of complex clients and legal issues, and I was armed with exactly half of a law school education to use against the venerable professional prosecutors of Cook County and one of the largest and most powerful law-enforcement agencies on earth, the Chicago Police Department.

What could go wrong?

There were three senior APDs assigned to that room when I interned there, because the caseload was massive. Each PD averaged 125 active cases at any given time, sometimes carrying as many as 150. The judge was evaluated by his superiors based in large part on the number of case dispositions ("dispos") per month, so there was constant pressure to bring each case to its conclusion. The personalities of the three PDs were so different from each other that watching them work was like a master class in the social and professional dynamics of meeting clients and presenting before the court. Whether intentionally or not, they each had a vibe that permeated their work: One was an older gentleman with a haggard appearance that he played up in his role as overwhelmed public servant and advocate for the poor (he later became a judge); one had a very polished appearance and demeanor that he used to convey a sense of calm professionalism that, given the circumstances, was often compared to the musicians who played on the deck of the *Titanic* as it sank; and one was a younger middle-aged woman whose slight stature was pronounced enough to be visually defining, which likely caused her to be generally underestimated, and certainly gave her a chip-on-her-shoulder attitude in dealing with all the crap that came her way. Aside from wonderful practical lessons that guided my career literally from its inception, they taught me the necessity and art of growing a thick skin. They were a motley battle crew in a boiling cauldron of underclass problems, and I was their wet-behind-the-ears note-taker and guardian of the calendar book.

As a "seven-eleven," I was able to read police reports. Lots of them. Given the caseloads of the attorneys in my courtroom, as well

as the monthly turnover of dispos and new arraignments, the extra
assistance requested by attorneys in other courtrooms, and my own
curiosity regarding heater or unusual cases being handled throughout the office, I could read upward of a thousand police reports each
month. The main ones were the arrest reports, supplemental incident
reports, general progress reports, and the forms that were used for
specialized purposes like evidence collection or inventory reports.
They were especially interesting if there was a section for the officer
to write a narrative. Fill-in-the-box information was important and
would be pored over in the process of evaluating consistencies of the
case narrative or devising investigation and litigation strategy. All
the details had to be reconciled with the process, conclusions, and
charges. I became very familiar with the standard tone, content, no-
menclature, and vernacular used in the industry of systematic arrest
and prosecution in the city of Chicago. Respectfully, I thought it was
a failing of the office that there wasn't a system in place to ensure that
cases were reviewed by more than one attorney, but I understood it
was primarily a function of caseload and also respect. Besides, any
time an attorney wanted a second set of eyes on a given case, all they
had to do was ask a colleague; despite the pressures and time constraints, almost everyone was happy to oblige.

While I was reading through the reports and files for the active
cases of the three attorneys for whom I was interning, I found the
gun case. The defendant was out on bail, and the attorney handling
the case had marked it for a guilty plea on the next appearance. According to the reports, an anonymous caller dialed 911 to report a
group of gang members having a meeting on the street, and the police sent a marked patrol car. This struck me as odd for two reasons:
First, there was no information at all about how exactly someone
would know that a group of people standing and talking on the street
were gang members having a meeting; and second, if the report had
specifically alleged gang activity, why hadn't the police sent one

of their specialized gang units instead of a blue-and-white? I turned out to be wrong about both instincts, as interns often are, but my curiosity served the purpose that the 711 program intended.

This is the dilemma for police: citizens generally want them to be proactive in preventing crime, but the Constitution imposes certain constraints on law-enforcement interventions. The balance is meant to be drawn intelligently and with the benefit of the doubt in favor of civil liberties, but there's not a bright line of clarity. Anonymous complaints generally require independent corroboration to allow the police to act upon them legally. From the defense perspective, as a first step, we try to verify that the police even received a real complaint at all. CPD always claimed that they erased 911 tapes after thirty days in the absence of a specific preservation order. That meant the recordings of all calls were erased for virtually every felony case in Chicago, because it takes longer than thirty days for the preliminary procedural steps to be completed to even charge someone with a felony, and even longer to invoke the formal right to counsel under the Constitution, and then have that lawyer file a motion for discovery, receive the materials, review them, and determine that the 911 tapes might be relevant, let alone critical. The police know it's unconstitutional for them to act on pure curiosity, or on baseless hunches, or improper motives such as racism, or reductive reasoning along the lines of "What else could it be?" It seemed to me that they guide themselves according to their own perceptions and beliefs about certain street activities. They will often claim to have received a complaint that spurred their actions, and then conveniently excuse the lack of proof of that complaint by saying it was anonymous, untraceable, or just "Nope, too late."

In any event, the defendant in my gun case was a gang member and had been talking to his associates on the street when the cops rolled up on them. A few weeks before his arrest in his then-current case, he had been shot. He was lucky to survive, taking bullets in the arm, leg, and chest. The chest wound was one of those miraculous "missed everything vital" types, and it had healed relatively quickly. But at the time of his latest arrest, he had one arm in a cast with a sling and one leg in a brace. He could barely walk by using a crutch with his good arm. He and the people with whom he'd been talking were standing just a few feet away from the steps to his apartment building when the squad car appeared, and everyone except him managed to run away before the cops got out. He didn't run because he couldn't run, so the police caught him and searched him and found a blue steel 9 mm tucked between his cast and his sling.

The arresting officers wrote in their reports (and later testified at the hearing) that they didn't know the defendant prior to his arrest, nor did they know the identities of the people who ran. They conceded that prior to stopping my client, they had not seen any display of insignia or behaviors that indicated the people were gang members. Their suspicion of gang activity was based on a combination of the alleged anonymous call, the area of the city they were in, the demographics of the people who were congregated (being young, male, and Hispanic), and the fact that almost all of them ran away upon the arrival of the officers.

On the one hand, there is a gang member with a gun on the street. On the other hand, even crediting the official version, the police used an anonymous, unverified complaint, together with blatant racial profiling, as the basis to stop and search someone whose actual activity at the time was simply talking to people while standing outside his house. I thought that the most likely explanation was that the cops saw a bunch of young Hispanic males in an area of the city that had gang activity (which is not specific, but not untrue either) and decided to check them out. Since the cops were driving a marked patrol car instead of an unmarked unit, a bunch of the subjects were able to run, and that only served to increase the cops' suspicions. At the time the case was active in court, there was still a US Supreme Court precedent that running away upon seeing the police was not conduct that legally gave rise to probable cause for an arrest or reasonable suspicion for a stop, but that changed a few years later. Regardless, my client had not run. As far as the police could observe, literally all he was doing before he was searched was exercising his constitutionally protected right of assembly with a small group of people, and the cops had no idea at the time who any of those people were.

Since my supervising attorney was recommending a plea, it presented sort of a "nothing to lose" opportunity, and I asked if I could file a motion to challenge the constitutionality of the stop and search. Of course that had already been considered by senior counsel, who was using the mere possibility of filing such a motion as leverage to get a more favorable plea offer. I suggested that we risk the negotiating leverage and go for a ruling that the gun was found as the result of an illegal search: If we won, the State would not be allowed to introduce the gun as evidence at trial, and without a gun, there's no conviction for gun possession; if we lost, the lawyer could just blame the over-exuberance of an intern, and still try for the same deal they would have gotten before my experiment. What really helped me was the fact that the defendant was out on bail. If he'd been in jail, he probably would have preferred to just take a plea and get it over with, but the luxury of fighting the case from a position of freedom was a major factor. When we explained everything to him, including the fact that I was a complete novice who had never argued a single case or motion in my entire life, he agreed to let me try.

He and I were about the same age, and I remember that his dad and my mom both came to watch the hearing. I called the officers as the only witnesses, and they stuck to what they had written in their reports. After the testimony, I gave a law-student dissertation on applicable law, which was unusual for routine hearings on these types of motions, but the judge found it refreshing. The judge was the Honorable Shelvin Singer, who was a professor and highly experienced jurist with a reputation for heavy sentencing. He agreed with me and granted the motion, ordering the gun to be suppressed from evidence at any eventual trial. The State took a continuance called an "appeal check date" to consider their options, but thirty days later they dropped the charges and my client walked free. I like to tell the story of my first win with immense pride, and mention my hope that I made as big an impression on that client's life as he made on mine, but usually the people who hear it are just angry about my role in putting an armed gangbanger back on the street. I try to explain that he didn't get the gun back and that he wasn't going to get a life sentence in any event, but most of the time they're still mad.

Every metropolis has problems with crime, but Chicago seems to have a particular reputation for violent crime. Our local media outlets print horrific headlines that do the macabre math when the wrong kinds of records are set over certain summer weekends: "85 Shot, 24 Fatally"; "At Least 106 People Shot, 14 Fatally, in Father's Day Violence"; "Chicago's Top Cop Tries to Deflect Blame for 110 Shootings"; and on and on, seemingly without end. Whether we deserve the reputation or not, at least some reliable statistics show that rates of violent crime (as defined to include murder, rape, robbery, and battery) per 100,000 people are dramatically higher than average in particular South and West Side neighborhoods, including Garfield Park, Washington Park, Englewood, North Lawndale, Grand Crossing, Riverdale, South Shore, and Chatham. Although statistics can be framed and selectively manipulated to support or dismiss almost any argument or conclusion, we certainly cannot deny the existence of violent crime on our streets.

Part of the reason this reputation resonates in modern times is that it's an echo of Chicago's gangster past. For the decades between the 1920s until at least the 1970s, Chicago was virtually synonymous with the infamous mobster Al Capone, the organized crime kingpin of the Windy City during that puritanical sumptuary known as Prohibition, the relatively brief period of US history when alcohol was illegal to manufacture and transport, which was intended to minimize, if not eliminate, possession and consumption too. Capone's influence and notoriety were celebrated and immortalized in folklore and films such as *Scarface, Al Capone, The St. Valentine's Day Massacre, The Godfather, Capone, The Scarface Mob, The Godfather: Part II* and *Part III*, and later *The Untouchables, The Revenge of Al Capone, Capone* (again), *The Lost Capone, Dillinger and Capone, Road to Perdition*, and *Gangster Land*, just to name a few. In addition to his gangster organization's use of extreme violence as they sought to control the black market of booze in the capital of the Midwest, he was also known for generous acts of local charity. Some people thought he represented the toughness of the immigrant and working classes in resistance to absurd governmental patronization, and, in a weird way, Chicago was (and still is) proud of him.

When Michael Jordan came along, for a solid decade or two he and the Bulls became the standard cultural touchstone for our city. Unfortunately, that glory has now faded enough that we are back to the criminal elements for our stereotypical identity. For a brief post-Bulls moment, our calling card returned to political corruption, that being as continuous a theme of local history as any, and featuring the high-profile arrests and convictions of governors George Ryan and Rod Blagojevich, as well as former Speaker of the US House of Representatives Dennis Hastert. But once again the popular and media reputation that precedes us has returned to violent crime, summarized concisely in a nickname that was conceived by Chicago-born rap artist King Louie, which he used to juxtapose the violence on our streets with the chaotic barbarity in one of America's most recent and enduring war zones: Chiraq. That moniker itself has since become controversial too, with some commentators expressing concerns that it can be used to stigmatize people, neighborhoods, or complex behaviors in a racist way, an issue that flared up and was examined at length when the term was chosen by Spike Lee as the title of his 2015 movie. However, there are some Chicagoans who think the Chiraq nickname represents a type of toughness of the streets in resistance to the hardships of inner-city life, and a certain part of Chicago is proud of that too.

All of which raises the obvious question: Why? Why is Chicago so violent? The answer has been elusive and is subject to seemingly endless debate. There are plenty of theories that it's due to some combination of factors that include poverty, gangs, drugs, guns, racism and segregation, substandard education, broken families and homes, recidivist felons, fetal alcohol exposure, and even our geographical location as a sort of hub in the urban center of America. Unfortunately, there has been no single, concise, tweetable bull's-eye of a consensus reason.

The real answer of course is painfully obvious to me: guns. An overwhelming amount of the violent crime in America generally, and in Chicago in particular, is gun crime. I really don't believe that Chicago is a wildly anomalous outlier in rates of gun crimes among American metropolis cities, but I know that America is a major global outlier among developed nations for gun crime on a national level. Americans can purchase and possess guns more easily than the citizens of virtually any other country on earth because of the literally fatal combination of the Second Amendment of the US Constitution, which protects "the right of the people to keep and bear arms," and the extraordinarily powerful special-interest political lobbying group the National Rifle Association, which works on behalf of the gun manufacturers and their toadying megalomaniacs.

Public defenders love the Constitution. We were created by the Constitution, although that was only recognized in 1963, after the slow drip of nearly two centuries of American history that passed without recognizing that a person's right to counsel in criminal prosecutions requires the government to provide attorneys to people who cannot afford to hire them. I dare suggest that many of us see ourselves as true patriots, putting our money where our mouths are in choosing a career that goes to the heart of protecting rights and freedom, while still being fanatically disliked, disfavored, and dismissed. When I told people that it was my great honor to work both for the government and against the government at the same time, some of them replied that they thought I was nuts—just a jejune liberal idealist who could not see the practical damage of my inherently oppugnant job.

The US Constitution was intended to establish and preserve individual liberties and restrictions on governmental authority in an unparalleled progressive liberal paradigm for its time. However, it was a product of its time, and like all things that are intended to remain vital and relevant over extended years and eras, it must adapt to survive. The world that existed at the time the Constitution was drafted simply did not include the technological, scientific, or social progress and pressures that have occurred over the centuries since its inception, so it's axiomatic that the thinking, rules, and provisions of the constitutional text didn't include them either.

Which is to say that unfortunately, even the Constitution has its flaws. Some of these flaws have been corrected over time, such as the Three-fifths Compromise, the initial omission of various fundamental civil rights, glaring exceptions of suffrage, and Prohibition. But other flaws persist. The right to counsel has been interpreted to begin only when charges are filed, meaning it excludes the most critical phase of all criminal prosecutions, the investigation. In practical terms, this interpretation means that people who are wealthy enough to afford private counsel can have the benefit of defense representation during the investigation phase, including questioning and interrogations, while people who are not wealthy enough to hire private counsel cannot. I want to doubt that the Constitution was intended to lock in such starkly disparate treatment of the rich and poor during the most critical interactions between government and citizen that any individual is likely to have in their entire lives, but given the reservation of certain rights for property-owning white males in 1789, maybe it was.

The constitutional right to bear arms was created in specific temporal and qualifying contexts. The amendment in which that right is recognized begins with a statement of a very specific purpose:

"A well regulated Militia, being necessary to the security of a free State . . ." In terms of the security of a free state, there is no convincing basis to believe that the founders of our republic intended to enshrine the ability of citizens to shoot each other—or government agents—just because there are sincere disagreements about the proper contours of governmental authority. The intent was to protect the territory from foreign invasion, which was necessary back then because our land was very big and our army was very small. We needed to call for backup in times of emergency. That is simply no longer true; our modern armed forces do not need, or probably want, help from the untrained, undisciplined, and unaligned masses. Which is precisely why, even if there were some absurd possible scenario in which the multi-trillion-dollar enterprise known as the US military actually needed help from Joe the farmer, Bob the accountant, or some random urban lothario, the key would be that such help is conditioned upon those volunteers being part of a well-regulated militia. This has been repeatedly interpreted to mean the National Guard. Come out for training, instruction, experience, and proven compliance with authoritative structure, and you may earn the right to be armed. Failing those prerequisites, you are simply a deadly loose cannon. How anyone could venerate the founders of America as brilliant visionaries, but simultaneously think that those same founders must've wanted every moron to be entitled to brandish deadly weapons, does not merely stretch the boundaries of common sense—it obliterates them.

Whatever a person's political stance is on the positives or negatives of gun ownership, or the constitutional basis for protecting the American right to keep and bear arms generally, nobody can deny that there has never been a shooting without a gun. Guns are easy to obtain, easy to use, intended to kill, and very effective for their designed purpose. They instantly confer the power of life and death on the person who is holding one, absolutely regardless of that person's intentions, intellectual capacity, emotional stability, discipline, or even attachment to reality. Public defenders handle tons of gun cases, tons of shootings, robberies, assaults and batteries, and in Chicago and other major cities, tons of murders. In stark contrast, I had exactly one case involving brass knuckles; a few with bats, clubs, and chemical sprays; a few with stun guns; and a small roster of cases involving knives. None of them caused mass casualties. We Americans suffer unconscionable tragedies in Columbine, Virginia Tech, Sandy Hook, Orlando, Las Vegas, Parkland, Uvalde, Highland Park, and many other places that are literally too numerous to count and mention. Yet still, a very powerful political lobby floods our national discourse about guns and possible remedies to gun violence with a virulent mix of disinformation, denial, and jingoistic pandering to a twisted and no-longer-relevant notion of frontier necessity.

"Gun control" is the generally accepted term for political efforts to limit the availability of firearms, either through regulations or bans that try to coexist with the constitutional baseline. A wide variety of approaches to gun control have been tried at federal, state, and local levels of government. One subset of these laws deals with the size, features, or capabilities of the weapons themselves, while another group applies to the people who are, or would be, gun owners, imposing background checks, carrying restrictions, and licensing requirements and exceptions. The practical effect of political differences and jurisdictional conflicts is a lack of uniformity and clarity when it comes to understanding exactly what actions are permitted and where they are allowed. The essential underlying rationale of legal gun possession is the human instinct for self-defense, a concept that's extremely easily understood; in contrast, the technicalities of legal gun ownership, possession, and use are very complicated. If there is no popular or political will to ban guns entirely, which there very clearly and sadly isn't, then a regulatory scheme that allows some people to have guns but prohibits them for others, no matter how well intended, inevitably ends up reflecting political considerations rather than practical ones.

In virtually every gun case I ever had, and in talking to other law-yers about their gun cases as well, whether the defendant was a gang member, a grandmother, a sports star, a veteran, or any sort of the everyday people in between, they almost always gave the same rea-son for having their gun: "I need it for protection." It's not the crazi-est thing I've ever heard, especially in Chicago, given the fact-based reputation of the city as a place with a relatively high prevalence of shootings, carjackings, gang violence, and robberies. However, even though there may be a basic rationality in a general desire for protec-tion, that alone is not a legal basis to carry firearms in Illinois. As a defense attorney, when your client tells you that the reason they were carrying was for protection, you probe the combination of motive and fact a little deeper, looking to build any possible affirmative or direct defenses on a foundation of truth.

Self-defense can be a bit more complicated than one might think, with filters that may apply such as initial aggressor determinations, attenuating circumstances that can create a duty to retreat, require-ments of commensurate force, questions of reasonability in percep-tions of fear and urgency, stand-your-ground laws, or castle doc-trines. Still, defense analysis often starts with self-defense since it's both an area of relatively broad legal protection and is likely to be the most relatable narrative for other people to accept. Additional justifications may be found in the reasonable use of force to defend other people or personal property. Sometimes there are defenses to explore based on creative interpretations of statutory language, such as whether or not a weapon was "immediately accessible" to the person charged with possession of it. For a long time in Illinois, there was at least one appellate precedent where a conviction was overturned for a man who had a gun under his seat as he was driving his car, because his attorney was able to prove that the man was too fat to have been able to reach it while actually seated in the vehicle.

As a public defender, you almost inevitably find yourself having these exploratory conversations in the lockup, patiently guiding your client through varying thickets of technicalities. Where the client's train of thought was simply a general desire to protect themselves from potential criminality on the streets of Chicago, or even something far more immediate like gang threats at their school or home, you are forced to advise that the law is designed to prevent defenses like that from being able to prevail. Some of them accept your guidance, while others reject it with sneering disdain. Prepared with any number of citations and examples, once the academic particulars of your counsel is exhausted, you may rest on the platitude "it's complicated," hoping against hope to end things gracefully. More than a few of the streetwise slicks don't let it go so easily, giving you a deadeye glare and a few seconds to soak it in before they sum up their own body of experience with some form of "No it ain't."

There's also that select group we meet who are definitely part of the problem. Aggravated discharge of a firearm was just about the worst charge to see on a new client sheet; armed robbery was up there too. For almost anything else—up to and including murder— there was at least the possibility of some backstory or detail that could explain, however bizarrely, that the crime was an act of human weakness, as opposed to something predatory. Even when someone's failure of self-control produced an awful result, I could try to understand what happened as the product of the abyss of mental disorders and illnesses that we stared into every day. But people who took guns and went hunting for other people they didn't know, without regard for the value of the humanity of their victims, those were the most difficult to represent. Not only because their actions were such grave offenses, but also because so many of them clearly embraced a persona of maximum interpersonal aggression. From the moment I called out defendants' names at the cell doors for our initial meeting and consultation, the way that they responded could tell me something about the person I was about to meet. The general attitude was usually appropriate for the routine of the moment, but the predators don't really turn that setting off. I certainly became aware of that very quickly when I was locked in a room with them.

At least criminals are just criminals; they've made no promises to anyone. They are what they portend to be, whether by necessity or avarice. Some of the arguably worst shootings in Chicago history were actually committed by the police. Not worst in terms of body count, but in terms of social impact and legal precedent.

Dr. Martin Luther King Jr. was assassinated by James Earl Ray on Thursday, April 4, 1968. On Friday, April 5, there were mass outbursts of emotion in more than a hundred cities across the United States, including Chicago. Any term used to describe that activity is loaded for potential conflict, but the common choices included civil unrest, protests, demonstrations, and riots. Undeniably, the anger in the streets turned to destruction and looting, particularly along a stretch of Madison Street to the west of Chicago Stadium, the old-fashioned brick barn that preceded the United Center and unofficially marked the end reach of "downtown" in that direction and the beginning of the West Side. In response, on April 6, Mayor Daley coordinated with President Johnson to organize a combined force of over ten thousand police officers supplemented by over eleven thousand soldiers from the National Guard and the regular army to be deployed on the city streets. By the end of April 7, there had been over two thousand arrests, more than five hundred reported injuries, and at least nine deaths.

The *Sun-Times* undertook the effort to investigate and report on the deaths, apparently recognizing the humanity in the cost that was paid by some for the murder of Dr. King. One of the reporters they sent was Ben Heineman Jr., a graduate of Harvard, Oxford, and Yale School of Law, who was also a Rhodes Scholar, law clerk to Supreme Court Justice Potter Stewart, and a future assistant secretary for policy at the Department of Health, Education and Welfare, as well as senior vice president and general counsel for multinational conglomerate General Electric. He and his partners began the same way public defenders do—with the police reports—because the information provided by the police establishes the outlines of things they are committed to on paper, and the first thing to do is to establish whether or not the official narrative makes sense.

Immediately interesting was the fact that four of the shooting deaths on Friday, April 5—approximately half the total of all the deaths—had occurred very close together in the 4100 and 4200 blocks of West Madison Street, and all within a relatively narrow window of time from eight to eleven p.m. All four victims were young black men. Heineman cross-referenced the coroner's reports for each of the four, which revealed a pattern of matching forensic evidence in each case—each man had been killed by a specific type of shotgun shell that was loaded with buckshot, normally used for hunting large game, but for combat purposes is intended to increase lethality. A compelling witness was found: the wife of victim Robert Dorsey, who said the couple had been walking together in the area around nine p.m. when they decided to detour through an alley to avoid Keeler Avenue because they could see a group of police officers "firing rifles into the air." She heard a burst of gunshots that caused her to think a large volley of firing was coming from someplace nearby and felt her husband push her to the ground for cover. He fell on top of her. Gathering what she was seeing into something she could understand, her eyes found a bullet wound in his back and a gaping hole in his front. She felt the viscous warmth of his blood, seemingly all over her. She provided her detailed recollections of the physical stages and signs of his death, and estimated the time when it occurred. Her summary accusation was candid and general, not emotional or overly bold: "I don't know who did it, but I didn't see anyone shooting but the police."

Heineman pressed on and found multiple witnesses who had been in the immediate area at the time of the four killings. Each witness described seeing at least one blue, unmarked Chevy that drove through and stopped in the area several times throughout the night. There were four white male officers inside, each with shotguns, and they were firing directly into buildings without giving any warnings. The witnesses saw the shootings and knew where the bodies were found, so they used the term "killer squad" to describe what they had seen.

When the *Sun-Times* ran their report on Monday, April 15, with the headline "Story Behind Riot Toll: The Nine Who Died," they apparently calculated a meaningful difference between what their reporter had found and what they were comfortable printing, and described the deaths as a "mystery" that occurred in the midst of "mobs of looters." They did not run the "killer squad" quote. The issue was in broad focus: what were the police orders and actions? They quoted a police spokesman saying, "There were no blanket orders pertaining to firing, one way or the other," and a patrolman who told them, "We were told to use our own judgment." Whether political pressure or a sense of journalistic ethics were at the root of their reluctance, they dutifully reported that the police were "ordered to take aggressive action in arresting violators of the law."

Maybe the story created some heat, or maybe the whole situation needed to be addressed, but either way Mayor Daley spoke at a press conference later in the morning on the day the story ran, presumably to try to set the record straight about what the police orders had been, and to dispel any rumors that the Chicago Police were responsible for anything other than bravely and firmly facing the danger, effectively quelling the riots, and restoring order. In a spectacular political backfire, and perhaps one of the most unambiguously blunt and direct confirmations of police brutality ever to come from a non-Dixiecrat politician, Daley said the words that shroud his legacy in eternal infamy:

I have conferred with the superintendent of police this morning and I gave him the following instructions, which I thought were instructions on the night of the fifth that were not carried out. I said to him very emphatically and very definitely that [he should issue an order] immediately and under his signature to shoot to kill any arsonist or anyone with a Molotov cocktail in his hand in Chicago because they're potential murderers, and to issue a police order to shoot to maim or cripple any arsonists and looters; arsonists to kill and looters to maim and detain. I assumed any superintendent would issue instructions to shoot arsonists on sight and to maim looters, but I found out this morning this wasn't so and therefore gave him specific instructions.

There was sufficient evidence to establish probable cause that the Chicago Police formed a kill squad, went hunting for young black men, and murdered at least four people without any veneer of due process; heck there was a confession, from the mayor, at a press conference! But this was not the peak of the civil rights era—it was the dawn. Not only did all the authorities who could have done something about it just let it go, but they doubled down with institutional policies that authorized the use of deadly force against inherently nonviolent property crimes, including stunningly minor offenses like attempted burglary, as well as against actions that are not inherently crimes at all in a free society, like attempted evasion of the police.

Having faced no consequences for the open and practically celebratory police violence in 1968, the authorities in Chicago took things another step further in 1969, working together with the feds to eliminate Fred Hampton. That occurred as part of another mass shooting, with two killed and four wounded. The circumstances and facts of that event are almost too bizarre to believe, but they have been extensively investigated and documented in most material respects.

Fred Hampton was the twenty-one-year-old leader of the Illinois Black Panther Party (BPP) and founder of the Rainbow Coalition.

The Black Panthers stood for a variety of leftist beliefs that included a mix of extremist and basic progressive causes, including revolution against the American capitalist order, Marxism, Socialism, anti-Zionism, anti-fascism, anti-racism, Black Power, and the prevention of police brutality. The Rainbow Coalition was a multicultural mix of groups who also supported various left-leaning political movements. Generally speaking, the police did not like the Black Panthers. Neither did the FBI, whose long-tenured and controversial leader J. Edgar Hoover called them "the greatest threat to the internal security of the country," based on his assessment that they were "a violence-prone organization seeking to overthrow the Government by revolutionary means." Hoover was obsessed, and where his energy was directed, so went the FBI. He was particularly focused on preventing a coordinated movement among black rights parties based on his belief that they could foment a revolution that would threaten the established White Christian order of American government and society. One of his initiatives was to create the COINTELPRO program, which was a massive counterintelligence operation that used surveillance, infiltration, perjury, police harassment, and outright violence to overtly and covertly attack BPP members, criminalize their activities, frame them for various crimes, spread disinformation to discredit and demoralize them, and even kill them when law enforcement deemed it appropriate. He ordered his agents to "destroy what the BPP stands for" and "eradicate its 'serve the people' programs."

In November 1969, there was a wild shootout between Chicago Police and members of the BPP in which nine officers were shot, two of whom died. A member of the Panthers was also killed, and although he was shot by the police, another Panther was charged with his murder. Hampton was not in Chicago when that occurred, but as soon as he got back, the FBI coordinated with the Cook County State's Attorney's Office and the CPD to raid Hampton's apartment under the pretense of a search for weapons.

On the night before the predawn raid, a COINTELPRO operative drugged Hampton with secobarbital, a powerful barbiturate. When the SWAT team burst into his apartment just before five a.m., they killed Hampton's security agent, who was armed with a shotgun, and whose death reflex caused the weapon to fire one shot into the ceiling, which was the only shot fired by the BPP members who were in the apartment. Hampton was sleeping in his bedroom beside his fiancée, and he was so heavily drugged that he never awoke. Officers dragged the woman out of the room and executed Hampton with two shots to his head at point-blank range while he lay drugged in his bed; he had never moved, threatened the officers, committed any specific crime, or even regained consciousness.

The officers then shot four other Panthers who had been sleeping in a separate bedroom, unleashing a barrage of ninety-nine shots. Those four BPP members weren't killed, but they were seriously wounded, beaten, and then dragged into the street before being arrested on charges of aggravated assault, armed violence, weapons charges, and the attempted murder of the officers. The police used a press conference on the following day to announce that the arrest team had been attacked by the Panthers and had used reasonable force to defend themselves. Subsequent police statements commended the raid team for their "bravery," "remarkable restraint," and "professional discipline" for not killing everyone who was there. FBI documents that were apparently stolen during a burglary at a field office in Pennsylvania in 1971 included a written agreement between the FBI and the US deputy attorney general to conceal the FBI's role in Hampton's murder and the very existence of the COINTELPRO operation; during pretrial discovery for the subsequent civil rights lawsuit *Hampton v. Hanrahan*, the government handed over their copy of the detailed floor plan to Hampton's apartment. Taken together, the killer squad shootings in 1968 and the Hampton execution in 1969 were some of the biggest links that ever failed in the chain of trust between the police in Chicago and that part of the public who felt most threatened by them, doing damage that seemingly has never been fixed.

I know a woman whose father was murdered in a robbery that ended up netting the perpetrator about five dollars. It happened when she was in her early twenties, less than a year after the birth of her first child, and it occurred right in front of her family's apartment building, the only place they'd lived for her entire life up to that point. After his murder, she moved away and never went back; she just couldn't bear the trauma. She was close friends with my wife, who had a terrible battle with pancreatic cancer that she lost when she was forty-three years old. Since then, this woman and I have become close friends, too, having had the chance to open up to each other about our shared sense of loss and pain. She knew about my career defending accused violent criminals, but she didn't say anything to me about it for a very long time. It seemed to be her way of keeping an emotional cushion for herself, and a respectful distance from that part of me. Eventually, the moment arrived when curiosity got the better of her silence. The path of approach she took was to ask whether I could understand her fear and that of many other people who've been victimized by violent crimes.

I told her about the two occasions as a public defender that I was out on street investigations and got caught in gang crossfire. Each time, my first impression was that I was witnessing a traffic incident. When you aren't directly involved in an unfolding situation, events develop before you physically and mentally arrive, and as you enter the scene, or it presents itself to you, your understanding can be shrouded by your unawareness until something forces you to catch up to the moment. The first time it happened, I thought I was hearing a street race between reckless teenagers because I could hear tires screeching, engines and brakes surging and waning, and youthful voices screaming in Spanish, just out of view from where I was. My brain initially processed it all as the sounds and then the visuals of a car chase, as a van came careening around the corner with a sedan in hot pursuit. They turned away from me, which instantaneously reinforced my feeling of being an uninvolved observer, but also gave me a clear look at the passenger side of each vehicle; the van's sliding door was all the way open with a young man hanging out, and the car had a guy propped up on the window ledge of the front passenger door. Both were holding on to their vehicles with one hand, and holding large guns in the other, firing wildly at each other as often as the mechanisms would allow. Suddenly I saw it all in slow motion—light flashes as muzzle bursts, popping waves of air, whizzes of projectiles just inches from my head, shards of concrete bursting on the sidewalk at my feet. Reality hits, but with astounding delay, presenting itself as a question: "Is this real?" Some part of you searches for confirmation, lagging with disbelief, if only for a fraction of a second. By the time my ability to think rationally was able to overcome the barriers of shock, it was all over. I recall exhaling as if for the first time in my life, staggering to reestablish my presence in the world.

The second time was at a four-way stop sign. Off to my right I checked the car on the line there, to judge which of us arrived first, and caught a glimpse instead of what I thought was a particularly jarring rear-ender collision. Physically recoiling from the jolt that I had seen but didn't feel, it became immediately apparent this was no accident, as the car in back reversed and was used as a battering ram a second time, pushing against the locked brakes and smoking tires of the resistance offered by the car in front. This time I was in, forgive me, a really shitty part of town, and my instincts were far quicker to kick in. As the drivers jumped out with burners in hands and engaged one another in a volley of shots, I peeled *the fuck* out and was lucky to cross the intersection and their line of fire without catching any slugs. So yes, I know the feeling of being shot at, or at least of being shot toward. I know the feeling of lucky escape, of miraculous dodging, of dancing with the vagaries of fate. Due to the searing cruelties of cancer, I also know the feeling of capricious death, of crushing grief, and the twisting knife of life's cruelest blows. I wish I didn't, but I do. Definitely not the same experience as suffering the murder of a loved one, but undeserved fear and loss just the same.

One thing's for sure: the guns don't care who's pointing them, or who they're pointing at. What a grotesque madness we've created where gun manufacturers are allowed to simultaneously create and sell both the problem and the perceived solution, raking in the profits, shielded by ironclad political protection, all while the bodies pile sky high.

Somehow, I never found myself sitting across from any of them in the jail.

VIII. DOMESTIC VIOLENCE

I went to a client's funeral once. Well, his wake actually. It was an open-casket viewing at a funeral home instead of a church, but they still passed out those little prayer cards with a picture of a saint on one side and a psalm on the other. There was the option to go up and kneel beside the coffin and offer a prayer or last respects, but as a non-Christian, I thought it would be inappropriate if I did all that, so I just took a seat at a respectful distance and sat in quiet contemplation.

He was no child, but he was young at the time of his death, no more than mid-thirties. He had been a severe alcoholic and died from the complications of it. Liver failure, if I'm not mistaken. He had no wife or kids—at least none that I knew about—and didn't seem to have many friends either. Hardly anyone was there, but maybe that was just because it was lunchtime in the middle of the week. I saw his parents near the front of the chapel, but I didn't want to disturb them, so I didn't say anything to anyone. I just lingered there awhile observing his everlasting peace, reflecting on his probable regrets and the turbulence in his life that had brought him to our interactions, and of course said my own prayers for his soul. It was the last act of advocacy I could offer for my client.

It was his parents, in fact, who had brought us together. When people hear the term "domestic violence," probably the stereotypical imagery they conjure up is that of some guy beating his wife, but it encompasses a lot more than that. At the time I was assigned to one of my rotations through DV court, the cases included all the usual family connections you can imagine, and also stretched to cover both current and former dating relationships and residential co-inhabitants.

The DV calls also had cases alleging violations of orders of protection, or VOOPs. Orders of protection, known as OPs, were like restraining orders. Under certain circumstances, OPs could be obtained in civil court in very brief hearings that were allowed to occur without advance notice to, or even the presence at the hearing of, the person against whom the OP was being sought. The hearings did not require much evidence for an OP to be granted; in fact, they specifically dispensed with historical evidentiary standards in terms of both quantity and quality. Public defenders are not allowed in civil court, but prosecutors are, and they had an entire division that was dedicated to helping people obtain these documents that carried enormous power behind them. Prosecutors win the overwhelming majority of their cases even when there is a protracted process and thoroughly contested hearings, but against people who weren't even there and were not allowed to defend themselves at all? They set 'em up and knocked 'em down, and all the VOOP cases came to us in criminal court.

Violence is bad enough, but domestic violence is a separate criminal category because there is an added dimension of harm that occurs in our personal sanctuaries, whether those are the emotional sanctuaries of our closest ring of relationships or the physical sanctuaries of our homes. DV laws are intended to protect these as safe spaces, specifically because these are the places where we're at our most vulnerable.

Originally, the American ethos was significantly centered on keeping the State out of private affairs, trusting the church to provide more intimate guidance. Historically, the ecclesiastical answer to domestic tension has been "to cherish and obey, for better or for worse." This was likely based on a common thread of patriarchal religious belief that every man needs a place to take off the metaphorical mask that is worn professionally and socially so that he can vent the frustrations and stresses brought on by daily living. It wasn't exactly progressive psychology, but in the days before therapy and counseling, it was misguided acknowledgment of the need for an outlet to keep the devil at bay. However, modern application of human rights includes having women on an equal footing with men, so traditional interpretations of domestic tranquility aren't close to sufficient anymore.

As the grotesque realities of domestic abuse were increasingly exposed in parallel with various other campaigns for women's rights, people in power were forced to acknowledge the unique harm that can be caused by abuse that is practically impossible to avoid or escape, and can be diabolically designed to be a protracted campaign of sabotage, manipulation, and control. In that sense, DV absolutely takes on a different character of criminal conduct than whatever might be committed between strangers, and it makes sense to craft tailored approaches and tools for law enforcement and for victims. Unfortunately, as damaging to individuals and families as domestic violence can be, when political attention began to focus on this particular issue in approximately the mid-1990s, perhaps understandably, politicians' initial posture was to overreact with draconian legislation. I'm relatively sure that the people who were in charge of drafting the laws and setting the punishments for breaking them were reasonably well intentioned and well informed, but politics rarely produces the best results, and the process is absurdly easily manipulated by people with extreme views. What ensued was a near reversal of the presumption of innocence in favor of a massive arsenal of pretrial punishments.

To be clear, my perspective as a defense lawyer isn't that DV shouldn't be categorized differently from other crimes or that it should be deemed unworthy of tailored protections, but that the complexity should not be seen as a reason to decrease pretrial protections and the chance of a fair trial for the accused.

Regardless of politics or advocacy, rationally speaking, it's virtually indisputable that these are the exact type of cases where people have the greatest interpersonal emotional bias and ego-driven incentives to lie. The sad phenomenon of people who seem to constantly claim to be physically sick when they are actually healthy is common enough that most people not only know the word hypochondriac, but they know someone who fits the bill. In extreme cases, that can escalate into a mental disorder called Munchausen syndrome, and the obsession becomes a self-fulfilling prophecy. There is no corresponding word that I know of to describe people who enjoy playing the role of victim so much that they are willing to exaggerate and fabricate criminal accusations against others, but it really seems to be common enough that there should be one, and "liar" just isn't enough. Hyper-agonium, maybe? The various editions of the *Diagnostic and Statistical Manual* of the American Psychiatric Association have consistently included "fragile ego" as a symptom of narcissism. I'm not saying that all narcissists become complainants in criminal cases, or that all complainants were narcissists, but my DV rotations certainly gave me the strong impression that there was a major correlation. I saw many DV cases that were based on current or former roommates or exes making some sort of bitter threat against the other, or based on some extremely minor physical touching or confrontation, and the party who felt aggrieved decided to resort to the leverage or revenge of calling the police. A lot of ego is involved in disputes; people feel compelled to "win," and when situations spiral out of their control, they can do desperate things to match the fever of the moment.

The police departments in Cook County generally had internal policies that if they were called out on a domestic, regardless of whatever the circumstances were when they got there, *someone* had to be arrested. This was explained to me as being based almost entirely on the fear of some nightmare scenario, which had happened in the past, of officers deciding that a given situation was minor enough that they could leave without making an arrest, only to have it escalate into horrific or deadly violence when they were gone. Then there was the "Can't go home" rule, which mandated that anyone who was arrested for a DV case and who shared a residence with the purported victim could not return to that residence for at least seventy-two hours following the arrest. It was quite common for that rule to be followed by bail conditions that prohibited contact between the parties, including a requirement that they maintain a certain physical distance between them that was always much larger than the size of a standard residential property. And of course, an emergency OP would be issued as well. The hammer of presumptive punishment, and therefore presumptive guilt, fell extremely hard and fast on the people who were charged with DV offenses. This was especially problematic given the monumental number of cases that ended up not being prosecuted; it was very common for complainants to fail to appear in court at all. When they did appear, it was so common for calmer emotions leading people to change their minds about pursuing a conviction that a special type of hearing procedure was developed for it, where the State puts the "victim" under oath and makes them acknowledge their refusal to prosecute, primarily as a way of protecting the cops and prosecutors from allegations of negligence and bad PR.

The prosecution teams had these extra layers of DV personnel, including State's Attorney's Office and police department Victims' Services Advocates, Pretrial Services officers from the Probation Department, and concerned citizens from community interest groups, literally called "court watchers." With the notable exception of those cases where the alleged victim was an adult male, in which case they did not appear to give a shit, they all treated the decision not to prosecute a DV case as a sort of dramatic travesty, as though the obvious reality was that their "victim" was simply too emotionally scarred to withstand the withering pressure of answering questions or the psychological trauma of recalling the terror of their abuse. They seemingly never even tried to consider that they might be enabling manipulators and perpetuating victimization of defendants who were devastated by false claims. That's the ether of official self-righteousness. Those advocates, whose very existence assumed the truth of the victimhood proposition that was not yet proved, simply did not have any professional ethical constraints. Crucially, although they were allowed to speak on the record despite not being professionally licensed or sworn to an oath, they were not subject to any requirement that they only present information they reasonably believed to be correct or had investigated in any way. They never had to pay a price for being wrong, so they never bothered to weigh the consequences of their actions in any nuanced way.

The chief judges who were in charge of the courthouses where I worked were almost entirely very bright, caring, professional jurists who were imbued with a humanity that very clearly conveyed their concerns for fair treatment of the defense, despite the popular and political pressures that must have been a large part of their jobs. I could catch them in conversation in both formal and informal contexts, whether at a panel presentation or for a quick word in the back hallways and offices, and I would see and hear the solutions they would propose as they listened to concerns from both sides of the system and tried to ensure procedural ethics while also trying to prevent real-world disasters. They wore the crown of power in truly inspiring ways, and I got the sense that the system was in good hands, despite the kind of two-cent pessimism that permeates news cycles and editorial pages.

The same could not be said of many of the junior judges who drew the DV call assignments. Dedicated DV calls were initially all misdemeanors, so the judges were the less-experienced ones who had not yet gotten an assignment in the Felony Trial Division. Misdemeanor DVs that weren't plea deals were almost always jury demands anyway because that took the case out of the DV courtrooms; the defense bar did not trust the DV judges to be objective at all, since they faced intense pressure from those prosecution team clusters of "advocates." It was one thing for judges to tell career prosecutors that their case failed for lack of proof, but it was entirely different to attempt to explain to three or four social workers or untrained observers why it wasn't possible to believe all claims of victimhood all the time. Judges who were nervous about being reelected just didn't have the stomach for it. Most of the daily work in DV calls was formulaic anyway, with the professional shelter of bail conditions and plea deals that weren't subject to any real scrutiny by appeals courts. I'm pretty sure that when a new judge was assigned to a DV call, the chief judges would instruct them that their main job was to make sure that no complainant got killed, which seems valiant enough, but is far more appropriate for a cop instead of an impartial jurist.

There was one judge in particular who seemed to draw the DV call quite often when I was assigned there and with whom I had just a terrible relationship. Probably because our mutual distrust didn't begin in a singular incident or confrontation, I forget exactly how our friction started. It's entirely possible that I wasn't completely innocent since I was young and brash and could certainly rub some people the wrong way. In my own defense, so to speak, this judge was regarded by the defense bar as the single worst one at the courthouse where she worked, based on a noted track record of decisions that were rooted in a logic that only she seemed able to comprehend. One of her favorite things to tell people was that since she had managed to make a successful career for herself despite her unprivileged immigrant background, anyone could succeed in life regardless of their circumstances. It was this exact type of "extrapolate from an irrelevant sample of one" reasoning that typified her conceptual approach to her jurisprudence.

Her reputation preceded her, but despite the warnings, I do recall that I initially gave her the benefit of the doubt and the respect of the robe. She had made a name for herself with an important appellate victory in the field of immigration defense law, setting a crucial precedent (that has since been reversed) that a defendant could potentially get a new trial on the basis of ineffective assistance of counsel if the attorney in their criminal case failed to warn them that deportation was a possible consequence of certain pleas or convictions. She was relatively young for the bench, but her judicial/political star was on the rise. However, early on in our interactions, she took a personal shot at me when she interrupted a bond hearing to instruct the stenographer to go off the record so she could ask me if my curly hair was natural or if I had a perm. It wasn't intended to be flattery either; it was an attempted knock at presumed vanity, in front of my client and the court staff. I shudder to think what the modern repercussions would be if a male judge interrupted a hearing to ask a twenty-something female lawyer about her hair. Actually, crap like that probably happened many times in the past—my mom liked to tell a story of appearing for a hearing shortly after her bar admission in 1953, only to be screamed at by a judge who saw this woman at the podium and presumed that her firm had sent a paralegal instead of a "real lawyer"—but it did seem particularly ironic for that specific gender-based double standard to be ignored in DV court.

Tragically, fate brought together that judge, me, and my alcoholic client. Alcoholics, like other addicts, don't usually succeed in their first attempt to get treatment or to get well. For my client, it was obvious that he was suffering, and that his parents were suffering too, and that they were trying to save their son. Their efforts had led them through a civil order of protection, and when that was violated with a trespassing charge that my client picked up by simply going home while drunk, the whole mess landed in criminal court with me. I got the impression that his parents were at the end of their emotional rope, and that the prosecution advocates were horribly misguiding them by urging them to use the full weight of the criminal justice system to weaponize their efforts to get him treatment, without factoring in the damage that would inevitably be caused to their family relationship and their son's trust. I was really sad that his parents couldn't seem to understand that either. Maybe that's part of why I didn't talk to them at his wake.

During the time his case was proceeding, my client missed a court date because he was hospitalized. Being present for every court date is a condition of all bonds, and when someone fails to show up, judges routinely issue bond forfeiture warrants called BFWs. However, ninety-nine times out of a hundred, when the court is informed that a defendant is hospitalized, instead of issuing the BFW, they'll use a trick called entering and continuing the warrant so that it doesn't go live in any law-enforcement database. They use this professional courtesy when there's a legitimate reason for the defendant to miss court. However, they are far more likely to grant this grace to private counsel than to any public defender. What they usually do when a PD claims that his or her client is hospitalized is order a probation officer to call the hospital and confirm. Many judges understand that PD clients are not always reluctant to lie to their own attorneys about why they are missing court, but when one of these backfires, as it sometimes does, we are the ones left embarrassed and damaged in the eyes of the court.

So the case gets called by the clerk, and the relevant parties step up to the bar to face the judge. If the defense lawyer is standing there alone, that's the first thing to be addressed: "Counsel, where is your client?" Rare is the occasion when the defense attorney can inform the court that the defendant is hospitalized, and when challenged for proof, turn to the prosecution team so that they can have their complainants, who happen to be the defendant's parents, confirm it for the record. And even rarer are those occasions when the judge refuses to believe both the defense and the prosecution, but that's exactly what happened. As she was instructing the Pretrial Services officer to make the confirmation call, she also inquired into my client's overall compliance with the conditions of his bond and was informed that he was refusing to give consent for the Probation Department, which oversees Pretrial Services, to have access to his medical records, as was his absolute right under federal law (the Health Insurance Portability and Accountability Act of 1996, or HIPAA).

Thus began the single most bizarre and stupid exchange I ever had with any judge. On the record this time, she dictated her order that the sheriffs immediately send a deputy to my client's hospital room and force him to sign a consent form for the release of his medical records. My objections began in an unorganized fashion, spit out as they were with the incredulity of having never expected someone who could attain the status of "the Honorable Judge" to be so obtuse. What about his medical condition? What if he can't understand? What about his rights under HIPAA? She was furious at me, each sentence bringing an even harsher tone and more entrenched fervor as she flexed her autocratic version of the power of the bench, which was especially pronounced in setting the conditions of bond in DV cases. I finally broke, and as closely as I can remember my exact words, they were: "Do you even hear the words coming out of your mouth? *Forced consent*. That cannot possibly be legal. No other court but you would ever recognize that." The instant I uttered the words that made it personal, I was extremely lucky to avoid being held in contempt. Contempt can be direct or indirect, and direct contempt results in immediate jail, without any real chance to appeal. Holding a lawyer in direct contempt and sending him or her to the lockup was the one line that I never saw crossed between an angry judge and a PD, and that day only the power of my office protected me.

What happens in these moments of outrage is that the line assistant will run to get a supervisor, and the judge will call to consult their chief. We both followed those protocols, and somewhere in the hallways or the phone lines, a de-escalation occurred. The exact reasons are settled off the record, sparing whomever the embarrassment of a public shaming. I felt vindicated when the judge's order was revised by order of the court, as opposed to being done as the result of any further argument on the record, but extremists win the momentum of the moment by merely shifting the argument so far off any rational basis that just returning the framing to reality wastes the energy of the defense.

Naturally, she retaliated. On the next court date, as my client waited in the hallway for the court call to begin, the Pretrial Services officer informed the judge that he was still refusing to surrender his rights to the sycophants in the Probation Department before he had been found guilty of any offense. She wrote a note on a slip of paper directing the sheriff to take him into custody for violation of his conditions of bail. The deputy to whom she had given the note was an older lady who was just working Court Services to pad her pension; she was some combination of uncomfortable and smart, and she brought the note to me. I took it straight to my boss, expecting that the outrage of an extra-judicial arrest warrant could be used to file a complaint with the Judicial Inquiry Board that would suitably end the career of that wannabe despot. But again, I was in for a lesson rooted in the realities of the system, as opposed to the formalities of the rules. I was told that filing a JIB complaint might get a judge censured or suspended, but it would certainly stain my career. In the interests of not making enemies out of everyone who was in a position to adjudicate my motions and trials, I ate it.

My client's cases had not been resolved when he died. When the defendant dies in a criminal case before the matter is final, the prosecution dismisses the complaint, indictment, or information by saying "Cause abated, death suggested." Their phraseology is so cold that it doesn't even concede that death is certain. For my quiet but solemn revenge, going forward on the DV call, I took advantage of a procedural technique that allows the defense to have a judge removed from any case without even giving a reason as long as the motion for substitution of judges, or SOJ, is filed within the first thirty days of the first time the case appears before that judge. Filing an SOJ is a bit unusual because it can be seen as a slap in the face, but I began a practice of filing SOJs against that judge on every DV case as a matter of routine. Word filtered up to the chief judge that I was upsetting the entire call with my campaign, but she knew why. Not long after that, both the judge and I were taken off the DV call and reassigned.

Before I was removed, I was asked to participate in a few of those discussion panels where concerned members of the community can come and hear about the measures being taken to deal with domestic violence and voice their concerns. A representative of the Public Defender's Office was required to be there in case someone had questions about protecting the rights of the accused, but it always felt like there were very few, if any, of those people there. In the best-case scenario, we were window dressing, and in the worst-case scenario, we would be the stand-in piñata for an old-fashioned public hectoring aimed at abusers and those who dare defend them. In the brief time I was given to present defense concerns, I would do my best to explain how the appointment of the victims' services representatives caused immeasurable damage to the presumption of innocence that was really the key foundation upon which the whole system had been built. Especially when a given DV case included elements that are entirely common in criminal court such as mental illness or various language and cultural barriers that are inherent to immigrants, the advocates were absurdly out of their depth.

Out of all my thousands of clients as a public defender, I brought exactly one of them home with me for dinner, and it was a combination of these vagaries and my sense of injustice about his situation that led me to do it. He was an elderly immigrant from the former Soviet Union, charged with a VOOP against his even more elderly mother for the underlying offense of trespassing. They lived together in a very modest apartment, with fixed-welfare incomes and extremely limited resources to address the mounting medical challenges that came with advancing age. Mom was well over ninety, practically deaf, and didn't speak a single word of English. On one particular occasion when her seventy-something-year-old son was out getting her medication, she locked him out. Having forgotten his key and becoming increasingly concerned when she didn't open the door, he smashed the window on the door and let himself in. The neighbors heard the noise and called the cops.

The suburban police were reluctant to accept his explanation of the chain of events and didn't have an interpreter available from dispatch, so an advocate was called. Without speaking fluent Russian, the advocate deduced that the mother was afraid of her son and had tried to lock him out intentionally. Complaints for trespassing and criminal damage to property were issued, as well as an OP, all of which were written entirely in English legalese. Minor enough as the situation was so far, my client was released on a recognizance bond that didn't require him to post any cash but, as standard conditions, forbade him from returning to the apartment. Of course, immediately upon his release, he proceeded to go home, where the landlord (who was still upset about the broken window) had him promptly re-arrested for a VOOP and a VOBB (violation of bail bond).

My courtroom partner and I usually split new cases according to a rough estimate of caseload and even-odd dates, but when this client came along, I had an extra advantage in the form of a girlfriend whose native language was Russian. With her help, I was able to cobble together just enough words to form the basis of a rapport with the older man, and he took a shine to me right away. This only increased when I got special permission to bring my girlfriend to the jail as a translator for my client conference, and he and I could discuss all the facts and procedures in the comfort of the company of a sympathetic ingenue.

We didn't take his story at face value, but the sense of whether or not someone is telling the truth is informed in large part by the detail and depth of background or supporting elements that aren't necessarily essential to the main point being proffered. Not just what happened, but why and how it happened; maybe what it smelled like at the time, or what reminders were triggered by a sound, or the associations or distractions the protagonist connects with a moment in the timeline, and the inconvenience or emotion of those as well. So often, when someone is trying to lie, they just tell their story from point A to point B and regurgitate a time-worn trope of not being able to remember some or all of the panoply of detail surrounding the central events. In contrast, this man was able to provide an entire narrative of his life with his mother, their immigration together, their medical struggles, the points of conflict and cooperation in their daily routines, and the ways their backgrounds informed their current circumstances. He was over seventy years old and had no known criminal history. Of course, the permanent posture of law-enforcement authorities is that a lack of a known background doesn't prove a lack of criminal behavior, only that the information is incomplete and can't be trusted. They especially rely on this presumption of guilt for all immigrants since foreign country records usually can't be obtained.

The old-timer had a colorful vocabulary, a clearly educated frame of reference, and what seemed to be genuine concern for his mother. My girlfriend and I went to talk to her, too, and found she was experiencing some of the lapses of acuity that can emerge with geriatric bloom. Perhaps her own reticence of confrontation affected her perceptions, but our impression was that the extensive interdependence of mother and son together with her declining condition left her more afraid *for* her son than afraid *of* him. It could have been naive idealism, a sense of sympathetic cultural similarity, respect for the elderly, or just wanting to impress my girlfriend with my caring empathy, but when the jail kicked him out and the OP kept him away from home, I brought him to my parents' house to celebrate Hanukkah. He swapped latke recipes with my mother and was gracious to everyone, even the family members who maybe wanted to hear about my cases but not necessarily meet them.

Over the following weeks, we were able to get him access to social services that were not part of the criminal justice system, including temporary housing and medications through Jewish charities, as well as counseling in Russian. His cases never went to trial because his mom passed away not long after the holidays. I didn't go to that funeral because her son had her remains repatriated to Ukraine. He came by the office once to thank me for everything my girlfriend and I had done, then I never saw him again. I owe him an unpayable debt of gratitude though: at least in part because she had the chance to see how I handled my job, my girlfriend was impressed enough to agree to become my wife.

Cook County didn't pay us to philosophize, but it's impossible to work in criminal court every day without occasionally stopping to think about why tragic things happen. I found this to be especially true in DV court, where my public defender perspective led me to wonder about both the people I was defending and the system I was struggling against. It was not my job to judge people; frankly, it was generally very uncomfortable watching people who had earned the right and obligation to judge others while they were actually doing so. How much context is enough, how much wisdom and mercy is required to be able to say with confidence that someone fully understands a situation they weren't part of, weren't present for, and are prepared to issue verdicts and orders that will have permanent effects?

The dangers of a rush to judgment are more physical for some than for others. One of my worst DV cases involved a young couple who were fairly typical among the working poor that we represented in the PD's Office: the man who became my client worked irregular day-labor jobs whenever he found them, and the woman was a part-time student and full-time mother, relying on her family to help look after their baby while she studied. They had a small apartment in a low-rise building in one of the less-glamorous parts of Evanston, the kind of place that people regard as temporary until circumstances conspire to make it longer term than they intended. At least it was close to the train station and to the woman's mother's apartment, providing some measure of help as they worked to build their family and careers.

On a particular Friday evening after a short construction assignment, the man was paid his wages in cash and was invited to join the guys from the crew for a few beers. These were the days before ubiquitous cell phones, so the woman was left alone with their baby, wondering where her man was—until he walked in much later than expected, much lighter in the wallet than expected, and smelling like he'd been having a good time while she strained to keep things in order at home. The stresses of her week, and maybe even some that carried over from her entire life, bubbled over and she snapped. By her own admission, it is fair to say that she was very angry during the ensuing argument and was giving him as much grief as she could in terms of what she was saying and how she was saying it.

Neighbors reported that they heard the argument and let it go for a bit, given that it wasn't too unusual to hear spasms of domestic strife in a place like theirs. When the couple burst out of their apartment and got into a physical confrontation on the front lawn, somebody called the police. Somewhere in the storm of invectives she was hurling at him about how he spent their money, his disrespect for her time, and his overall shortcomings as a man, he decided that his best course of action was to leave. But she wasn't about to tolerate being left alone again and chased after him. Thinking that maybe he could mollify her by handing over what remained of his wad of cash, he tried just giving her the money. Incensed by what she perceived as being treated like hired help instead of a true partner, she began to tear the bills into shreds and throw the pieces at him. Instinctively and desperately, he grabbed her in a bear hug, trying to stop her from destroying the cash. He was focused on that effort and had his back toward the street at the moment the police pulled up.

This is as good a point in the story as any to note that he was about six foot four, 250 pounds, had been a linebacker in high school, was still very muscular from his construction work, and could be accurately described as a huge black dude. For what it's worth, his girlfriend was of sufficient height and build that she wouldn't be considered small by hardly any standards except when standing next to him. The combination of imagination and testimony paint the picture of what the police saw as soon as they arrived, and that was a massive guy literally manhandling a woman without much regard for anything else that was going on around them, including the arrival of the cops.

Police carry a selection of tools and weapons, a common one of which is called an ASP baton. ASP is the company that makes it; the baton is designed to be carried on a tool belt at a size comparable to a full tube of toothpaste, but with a flick of the wrist, it expands in length like a telescope into a steel bat the approximate length of a human arm. As the responding officers ran up behind my client, they said they were shouting, *"Police! Let her go!,"* perceiving an urgent crisis that demanded swift action. Among the many tropes that are repeated in police reports across jurisdictions and time, they always claim to have used "the appropriate amount of force that was necessary under the circumstances." What they did was started swinging with the ASP baton, first striking his back, then his legs, and as he went down, his head. He had enough strength and adrenaline in the moment to reflexively defend himself by raising his arms in a defensive shield, and then grabbing at the baton, trying to push the officers away. Needless to say, he ultimately lost the struggle to a team of officers and was subdued and arrested.

The cops are very well aware of potential lawsuits regarding use of force, so they did what most cops do: they orchestrated a completely ham-handed internal investigation to instantly clear themselves of any wrongdoing, and tagged the defendant with all the charges they could, including domestic battery, aggravated assault to a peace officer, and resisting arrest. The photos from these sorts of cases are usually simultaneously disgusting and morbidly hilarious because they show serious injuries to the defendant around virtually all parts of the body, almost always including the face, and then there are a series that the cops have posed for showing their bruised knuckles and scraped knees from where they kicked the shit out of the arrestee and are preparing to take their paid vacations and put themselves up for awards for bravery. The looks on their faces is like those pictures you sometimes see of some obnoxious asshole on safari standing over the carcass of whatever animal they've just bagged; the defendants' faces are almost always stunned and hollow, whereas the cops' faces are fiery with confidence and pride, usually barely containing their victorious smiles, but sometimes not. All defense attorneys have shared their disgust about not only these pictures, but also mock the boilerplate phrasing of the charges and reports, rearranging the wording to a new version that would at least be closer to true if it described how the defendant repeatedly attacked the officers' fists with his face.

This case had to be a jury trial for two reasons: First, it seemed like he might really be innocent, so that was important. But even that relied on claims of self-defense and defense of property; those are affirmative defenses, the kind where the defendant admits to the conduct that is the basis of the charge, but claims such conduct was justified by law. Those are always extra risky because you are admitting to the physical acts and then hoping that the defendant's perceptions and actions in the moment can be judged to have been reasonable from the perspective of analytical hindsight. Second, even for innocent clients in DV cases, the risk calculus is really severe due to the emotional nature of the events. Many judges will not rule "not guilty" in a DV case, period. They have the ability to err on the side of caution, and they do. The same is true for resisting arrest cases. The judge essentially has to call the police liars, and that is just not going to happen unless there is such irrefutable proof that the judge has no choice. That's why most DV and resisting cases don't go to trial, and of the tiny sliver that do, they almost always have to be jury trials. There was no good option to plead this one out, even though we were definitely afraid of the risk of going to trial. We knew we were in for a big fight.

Returning to a shockingly common theme that I personally saw repeated many times in my career, despite the overwhelmingly clear obligation to give the defense all the evidence in the possession of the police and prosecution before trial so that there is no such thing as trial by ambush, they withheld key evidence. Throughout all the months of pretrial maneuvering and calendars, they claimed there were no pictures of the defendant that were taken when he was given medical treatment after his arrest. Often times when a suburban department tries to hand over arrestees to the Cook County Jail, if the person is in obviously bad shape, county refuses to take them. This can result in weird timelines where an arrestee claims to have been injured during his or her arrest, but there is little evidence to corroborate those claims because the arresting agency just sat on him or her for however long they think is necessary for the person to stop complaining. When county says no to accepting them, then there is a period of a few hours where the defendant is taken to one of the pathetic hospitals on the Far South Side and given some form of barely cosmetic treatment before being rebooked. If a defense attorney questions the unusual delay between the time of arrest and the time of entry into county, it's dismissed as "we were busy."

However, in this case the defendant was so badly injured that they had no choice but to have him transported to Evanston Hospital relatively soon after his arrest, and when they were trying to justify their use of force, they'd sent a sergeant over to conduct the use-of-force review. The sergeant had snapped a few Polaroids of my client on a gurney, in a neck brace, his eyes deep purple and swollen shut, with blood all over his face from the lacerations on his scalp. They just never bothered to admit those existed, let alone produce them, until that sergeant was testifying before the jury. A moment like that in a jury trial, where a supervising officer admits there is evidence that has been withheld from the defense and is ordered by the judge to immediately go and get it, always makes the reveal that much more dramatic. When you can show the jury exactly what the defendant suffered, claims of self-defense make a ton more sense. On top of that, if the alleged victim testifies that the defendant only grabbed her when she began to destroy the money, which she did in this trial, then we can argue that seeing cash torn apart is an act that would cause most reasonable people to react; also, claims of defense of property work well too. I remember after we won, one of the jurors was an elderly black woman, and she came up to me and said that although she had no regrets about her verdict, she wanted to be sure that I would tell my client to keep his hands off women in the future (I gave her my word, and I kept it). I don't remember the exact settlement amount he got from the police, because civil suits are not handled by the Public Defender's Office, but I believe it was more than enough to relieve their financial stresses for quite a while.

With the benefit of a certain detachment, I sometimes wondered if the people who had lost their tempers within the confines of a relationship that had the greatest potential to affect their emotions were actually so bad. I often thought about the larger design at work that prevented our governmental resources from being used in a nurturing way rather than a punishing one. Living in the Midwest, I've heard my share of folksy idioms, one of which is that an ounce of prevention is worth a pound of cure. I started to think that there were common flaws in the people and the system I represented: overstressed, more reactive instead of proactive, having resources available but still disconnected from them by some combination of miscommunication and disinterest. Not truly evil, but just mismanaged, like schools that somehow fail to teach generations of students the art of note-taking and the skill of time management, and the fact that we need a license to drive a car but not to be a parent. Mental health came into focus as the possible key to preventing the traumas of historically tragically under-informed parenting and underdeveloped coping skills from being relentlessly passed forward, but for reasons I can only speculate are a combination of politics and money, there was never any emphasis on ways to structure a public system to deliver assistance as a preference to punishments.

I struggled through the political, emotional, and legal minefields of the DV call with the help of a great courtroom partner. She was a few years older than I was, and she could always help me see beyond my jaded sense that most people were exaggerating benign incidents to gain an advantage in their divorce or child custody cases, or that the busybody advocates were intentionally inflating claims that were inherently likely to be emotionally biased simply to justify their continued existence and expanding budgets. She was a great balance for my imprecise allegations of systemic failures, since very few people were willing to listen to a young male defense attorney try to articulate inchoate academic objections to a system that was attempting, however imperfectly, to fix massive oversights of the past.

It would be a few more years until some of my objections to manipulation in DV cases were proven by the Drew Peterson case just outside of Chicago. He was a police officer in Bolingbrook who was ultimately convicted of murdering one of his wives, remains the only suspect in the murder of another of his wives, and was later convicted of trying to hire a hit man to kill the prosecutor who had put him away. Between 2002 and 2004, there were no less than eighteen documented calls to police from the Peterson home regarding incidents of alleged domestic violence. Although these occurred at the exact same time that I was being told there was a firm policy of making arrests on every domestic call, Peterson was never taken in even once. The term "home cooking" is the euphemism for friendly evidence manipulation and is usually seen most often in suspected drunk driving cases involving a police officer; officers will wait many hours to collect breath or blood samples, or even just let it go completely if the officer has sufficient clout, like when Chicago Police found their boss Superintendent Eddie Johnson passed out behind the wheel at a stop sign one night and just let him drive home instead of testing him at all, and then when the inspector general who was tasked with investigating that incident took more than six months to complete his report to the mayor. It was painful, but not really all that shocking, to learn they used a little home cooking to let one of their fellow officers murder at least one woman, probably two.

Obviously, the existence of at least an attempted, and likely actual, serial killer in a police uniform is extremely rare, to say the least. We wouldn't have gotten cases like Peterson's in DV court anyway. We didn't see the worst abuses while we were working the DV call because charges like grievous bodily harm and murder were taken out of DV court and sent to the specialized felony courts. Undoubtedly, governmental leaders were using the DV system to try to correct for some obvious historical shortcomings while they worked to figure out the right balance to protect the public and the rights of the accused. I can't speak for the Public Defender's Office now in the same way I once did, but I clearly remember not being alone in the strong belief that the tremendous powers of the court were too often brought to bear on the basis of weak and obviously biased information and entrenched stereotypes, forcing us to waste valuable time and resources defending people from subjective offenses and hurt feelings while some far more pressing problems went unchecked. Watching my clients and their loved ones literally die under the strain of certain DV court processes while the system simultaneously failed to use the tools it had created to possibly save people's lives certainly left a very bitter taste.

IX. DRUGS

About a third of all felony cases in Chicago's criminal courts are drug cases. The correct legal terminology for a drug charge in Cook County is "possession of a controlled substance," or PCS. Possession is the lowest-level drug charge and is referred to as "simple possession," even though it carries a possible prison sentence, depending on the type of drug involved.

Possession with intent to deliver (PCS w/I) and delivery of a controlled substance (DCS) are more serious charges, and each category has escalating penalties for larger amounts. The majority of PCS cases are for crack cocaine, with heroin coming in a distant second. Cannabis cases aren't felonies unless the weights were relatively high (over 30 grams), so we had comparatively fewer of those in the felony courts. There are a wide range of drugs that are illegal to possess, manufacture, and deliver, but coke and heroin are the most common basis of felony cases in Chicago for two reasons: those drugs are the principal business enterprise of the street gangs, and the street gangs are the principal business enterprise of the police. If someone wanted something more exotic like ecstasy or mushrooms, they had to go talk to their favorite bartender or DJ, because inner-city street gangs were not the place to get those.

Gangs sell drugs in housing projects, abandoned buildings, and on the streets in "open-air markets" that they establish in the areas they control against interference from other gangs. They don't bother with elaborate packaging; it's not a small zip-lock bag or logoed envelope, like you see in the movies or on TV. Most of the time each crack rock is wrapped in a small square of plastic wrap that's been twisted shut, and someone has drooled all over it because it's extremely common for dealers and users to hide rocks in their mouths. Crack cocaine is cocaine that's been diluted by mixing it with various preservatives and then cooked into sort of a solid instead of the purer powder form that's more expensive. I say "sort of" because even after it's cooked, it has the consistency of a tiny lump of buttered sugar. It's very easy to break apart, and after a few months in an evidence locker, depending on what it was mixed with, it melts into a gross yellowish-brownish liquid if it isn't refrigerated. For some reason, heroin—or "herr-ron" as it was pronounced by virtually every gang member and junkie I ever met—is almost always a yellowish powder wrapped in foil.

Gangs sell weed too, but mostly in nickel and dime packs, meaning for five or ten dollars. The weight of those is small enough to be a misdemeanor instead of a felony. Catching a weed misdemeanor from the Chicago Police was like getting a traffic ticket from them anywhere except on Lake Shore Drive; it wasn't very likely to happen because it wasn't worth the officer's time to do the paperwork and "jam someone up" unless the violation was particularly flagrant, the cop had a specific need to make numbers like a quota or a looming performance review, or the person was rude or had done something else to warrant the effort. From what I heard, most tactical or gang officers were more likely to use the weed they found as leverage to intimidate people or recruit informants rather than do the paperwork on a misdemeanor. Besides, whenever someone was charged with felony and misdemeanor drug charges together, it was common practice for the misdemeanor counts to be dismissed when the case was sent to the Felony Trial Division.

The distributors seem to be extremely careful in maintaining the consistency of their product weight; virtually every rock or dose weighs exactly 0.1 grams. In the thousands of drug cases I ever had or discussed with colleagues, it was far less common to have a case where the Illinois State Police crime lab weighed out a rock or packet at 0.2 grams, and I never saw one at 0.3 or more. Most Americans have no clue about metric weights, so I always described it as one tenth of a sugar packet and told them that if they wanted to know how small it really was, the next time they buy coffee at Dunkin Donuts or Starbucks, try to divide the contents of a single sugar packet into ten equal parts, and consider one of them. It's extremely tiny and as light as air. We send an endless parade of people, mostly underclass people, to the hell on earth of imprisonment for the equivalent of a few specks of dust—that's what human life is worth in America.

Street sales usually involve a small crew of the youngest gang recruits hiding a stash somewhere disguised as garbage; in my experience, it was overwhelmingly fast-food containers and cigarette boxes. Occasionally someone would get creative and use a broken fencepost, a power box, or the wheel well of a parked car. One guy keeps a few packages on him at a time, often in his mouth, and another dude takes the cash and signals the holder to pass however many "jums" to the customer. Lookouts are positioned on corners, on rooftops, on elevated porches, or basically wherever they can see vehicles approaching and holler out some crude signal. It's not a foolproof or highly professional operation, but they manage to conduct their business pretty effectively.

Understanding these patterns very well, the Chicago Police generally concentrate their anti-drug efforts in and around the gang-controlled markets. They designate those markets and certain junkie hangouts as places of "known narcotics activity," and direct tactical squads to conduct a much higher volume of patrols, street stops, and surveillance operations in those areas than they do elsewhere. Sometimes they organize sophisticated operations with informants and undercover buyers; other times they just park an "unmarked" cruiser someplace where they think it isn't too conspicuous, and the two or three officers watch a suspected street dealer from their car or someplace nearby on foot.

The problem with those less sophisticated surveillance operations is that virtually everyone who lives in those high-patrol areas is extremely familiar with what unmarked cars and plainclothes cops look like. In Chicago, the tactical units were not in police uniforms per se, but utilized a sort of de facto uniform consisting of blue jeans and ballcaps, covered by large black tactical vests with gear harnesses for their radios and various less-lethal weapons like ASP batons, Tasers, and sprays. They would display their badges as giant chain necklaces or on a conspicuous belt clip. Their cars were lower profile than patrol units, but could be spotted a mile away by anyone who was interested because they always used the same models of American-made cars that were painted some dull monochrome gray or green, with heavy-duty all-black tires without hubcaps. The license plates were printed in standout green lettering that was a string of numbers preceded by the letter "M," which stood for registration to a municipality; then they graduated to "MP," for Municipal Police. Very few other cars in Illinois besides patrol cars could have those. The cars also had large police-only crash cages on the front bumper. The same cars would go back and forth in their assigned zones over and over again, swooping up the curbs or against the flow of traffic, and two or three officers with aggressive demeanors would jump out and grab their next street-stop target and put them "on the car" in the well-known sprawled pose that creates control and submission. Everybody knew who they were the moment they got on the block.

Despite being instantly recognizable in a potentially lethal game of hide-and-seek, officers routinely claimed that they were able to witness one or more hand-to-hand transactions of "an unknown amount of USC" (United States currency) in exchange for a "small item," and based on seeing that suspicious activity, they "approached to conduct a street interview." Their reports would almost always contain the same boilerplate language repeating those lines: "an un-known amount of USC" that was exchanged for a "small item" that would later be determined to contain a "rock-like substance" that weighed 0.1 grams. I was always deeply skeptical of police claims of having witnessed the particulars of a hand-to-hand transaction, and I wasn't alone among those of us on the defense. Common sense is easily applied to understand how difficult it is to see people hand things to each other when they are as small as folded money or a 0.1 gram lump of anything, and the exchange is being done using tech-niques that have been developed and tested over time for the specific purpose of evading prying eyes. Not all handshakes are as elaborate as the choreographed celebrations of a touchdown or a home run, but they can be as slick and smooth as a magician's, and as the old saying goes, the hand is quicker than the eye.

Crucially for this high-stakes cat-and-mouse routine, the cops are savvy enough to know the general contours of the constitutional re-quirements of probable cause and articulable reasonable suspicion, so they work to meet those thresholds. There is a lot of gray area in the law about what kinds of behaviors legally justify searches and seizures. Certain behavioral patterns do give rise to proper police action, but cops are supposed to be constitutionally restrained from just stopping and searching someone based on a hunch or a feeling, or based on the way someone looks, or profiling people based on race, age, and what part of town they are in at what hour of the day. Experienced officers know that generally speaking, hand-to-hand transactions where they cannot see what's being exchanged are not legally sufficient grounds to stop someone and search them. How-ever, the cops aren't idiots either; they know damn well what's prob-ably going on, and they want to make arrests and protect themselves and the cases they make.

In reality, the police see *something* or *someone* they find suspicious, and they swoop in to investigate. Nobody can deny that the police are patrolling with great intensity to find drug activity, some dealers are lazy or bad at their jobs, most users are careless and reckless, and the police certainly do catch people off guard sometimes. There's a certain logic and structure to what both sides are doing. Regardless of any possible criticisms of the police, they use a literal army of officers and a vast array of equipment and technology, and some of what they do is highly sophisticated. Aggressive officers rely on every tool they have to do their jobs, and they do them very well. However, only the naive or the evil doubt or deny that some of those tools are not entirely legal, including the very simple and very time-tested familiar tool of just plain lying. Thus was born the drop case.

"Drop cases" are those absurdly common instances where officers claim that they were approaching someone to conduct a "field interview"—that is, just to talk and totally not to stop and search that person—when their target simply dropped drugs on the ground in plain view before the police needed to take any official action. Police use this story to claim that they did not conduct a search in order to make an arrest, and thus the main defense in all drug cases—that the search which led to the discovery of the drugs was unconstitutional—cannot apply. It's the childish "I found it" explanation for drug arrests. In virtually no other context in life do we accept this wishful serendipity as an explanation for someone having something they shouldn't have, but the police not only use this ridiculous line with regularity, they also often write it in their reports in very standard fashion, including the detail that the dropper didn't even try to run. An unwritten tradition of Chicago courts used to see a fair number of judges remove drop cases from the system at the preliminary hearing stage by entering a finding of no probable cause to charge a felony, without giving any public explanation except a raised eyebrow that never made it into the official record. It was the old-school way of dealing with what the veterans called "testi-lying." Still, many other judges let them through, leading to a classic case of the cop's word against the defendant's. In other words, slam-dunk convictions.

What really surprised me was that no matter how many cases

I won by proving that windows were opaque instead of transparent, or by winning a pretrial motion to disclose the surveillance location that allowed us to prove that an officer who testified that he witnessed a transaction from twenty feet away was actually more than ten times farther than that, or by bringing out blatant contradictions in the police reports or testimony—and I won hundreds of them, and career PDs win many more—there were always people who flatly refused to believe that officers lie in order to make arrests or win convictions. No amount of direct or empirical proof could open their minds to the possibility—let alone the mathematical and human inevitability—that some police abuse their power. On those rare occasions when the skeptics were pressed so hard that they felt backed into a corner about it, they would whip out the same contradictory bargaining tropes of "a few bad apples" or the most common: "Who would believe anything a druggie says?" They made their last stand on "Why would the police lie?" as though no possible motive were conceivable. After all, we weren't usually saying that the defendant didn't possess drugs or use them, just that the way in which they had been caught amounted to a violation of personal constitutional rights. Such violations form a type of defense because evidence that is collected by violating someone's rights gets excluded from trial and the case cannot proceed, even though the fundamental allegation isn't negated. Of course, nobody wants to believe a drug user or their attorney; rejection of our word is reflexive, practically axiomatic, due to the presumption that people will say anything to avoid going to prison. Very few people stopped to think that, conversely from the somewhat sophisticated officers, the defendants generally had no clue about the details or intricacies of constitutional law and were simply pointing out how the actual events leading up to their arrests were completely different from what was written in the reports or given as testimony.

The people who refused to see, believe, or just acknowledge that a dishonest element of law enforcement exists didn't have to take my word for it, or the word of my colleagues or clients; they had to ignore a nearly continuous chain of federal investigations and convictions of corrupt officers in and around Chicago. The first one to occur during my time in the PD's Office was in 1996, from the Austin District on the West Side. CPD Internal Affairs and the FBI received complaints about tactical officers robbing people of cash and drugs, and began an undercover sting investigation called Operation Broken Star. The investigation lasted for two years and resulted in the arrest and convictions of seven officers from the Austin tactical squad. Apparently, a member of the Conservative Vice Lords street gang managed to infiltrate the police department and get assigned to tactical, whereupon he began to recruit other officers to assist in his scheme to shake down dealers who belonged to his rival gang, the Four Corner Hustlers. The crew of crooked officers were caught robbing and extorting alleged drug dealers on at least twelve separate occasions throughout the operation. The feds cataloged over $65,000 taken, found un-inventoried drugs in the personal police-station lockers of five of the cops at the time of their arrests, and indicted the officers on twenty-one counts, including conspiracy, robbery, gun and drug crimes, and civil rights violations that resulted in convictions and sentences ranging from 5 years to 115 years in prison for the infiltrator.

A strikingly similar pattern of behavior was happening at the same time in the Gresham District, which came to light in 1997. Three tactical officers were convicted in a joint FBI and CPD undercover sting, this time called Operation Betrayed Trust. They were also indicted on charges including robbery, conspiracy, drug possession with intent to distribute, civil rights violations, and illegal use of firearms. Their scheme relied on a local drug dealer who set up his competitors or enemies for the tactical crew to rob of drugs and cash, after which the four of them would split the proceeds. The feds had audio, video, and the testimony of the mistress of one officer, who was riding along in the squad car with her on-duty lover, and who testified that she personally witnessed approximately twenty such robberies of cash and drugs over two years. Caught on tape was this gem of a quote from one of the dirty cops: "We so fuckin' smooth, it's ridiculous." One of the jurors was interviewed by the press after the convictions and succinctly touched on the undercurrent that concerns the defense every time: "You tend to wonder, how often does this happen?" During these same years and apparently for many years leading up to them, Officer Joseph Miedzianowski of the gang crime unit was operating an interstate drug ring between Chicago and Miami, robbing alleged drug dealers, lying in reports and testimonies to fix cases, harboring a fugitive who was wanted for murder, and ratting out fellow officers to street gangs. He was finally convicted in April 2001, with his sentence of life without the possibility of parole recognizing that he had committed his crimes throughout almost all of his twenty-two years on the force. Out of all the possible nominees, it's Miedzianowski who is generally referred to in the media and academic reviews as "the Most Corrupt Cop in the History of the Chicago Police." When the feds executed a search warrant on Miedzianowski's home, they found thousands of Internal Affairs documents that were just taken and buried. A federal prosecutor named Brian Netols testified during the Miedzianowski case that he believed the Chicago Police Department was involved in a RICO conspiracy with Miedzianowski, and that an unwritten "code of silence" was involved in all eighteen criminal trials of Chicago Police that he'd prosecuted, including when he served as the lead prosecutor in Operation Broken Star.

Years later Brian and I worked together at a private firm that represented corporate clients in internal anti-fraud investigations, and we had a chance to discuss our mutual disdain at what had occurred on the streets of our city, and to marvel at the odd parallels we had unknowingly shared in the common cause of proving police misconduct despite the vastly different roles of our offices. He told me I probably couldn't believe the true scope of the crimes he'd seen, only a fraction of which the US Attorney's Office had been able to prove in court. I admitted that I'd never know but said I could probably imagine. In return, I told him he probably couldn't believe how many complaints we PDs heard from our clients about the activities of the Chicago Police. His reaction struck me as quintessentially professionally prosecutorial—not at all sympathetic to either side, just disgusted at the swamp of criminality and especially bothered by those who had taken an oath to uphold the law and then betrayed and exploited it.

In addition to the Austin, Gresham, and Miedzianowski affairs, throughout most of the 1990s Sergeant Eddie Hicks was running a four-man robbery and extortion crew within the CPD Narcotics Section. According to his federal indictment, from the early 1990s until after Hicks's retirement in 2000, the Hicks crew conducted warrantless, unauthorized drug raids and traffic stops of alleged drug dealers and kept whatever drugs, cash, or weapons they found without arresting those from whom they'd allegedly recovered contraband. They stole thousands of dollars in cash, multi-kilogram quantities of cocaine, hundreds of pounds of marijuana, and an unknown number of firearms, and were charged with RICO conspiracy, narcotics conspiracy, extortion conspiracy, possession of a firearm in furtherance of a narcotics conspiracy, and theft of government funds. His three co-conspirators pled guilty in 2003, but the sergeant fled on the eve of trial and managed to stay on the run for almost fifteen years until his arrest in 2017 in Detroit. Despite supposedly being the target of an international manhunt, during his time as a fugitive, Hicks was able to sign documents transferring property to his son, also an officer with the Chicago Police, as well as receiving and signing over $300,000 of his police pension checks so that his wife could deposit or cash them.

Right after Miedzianowski and the Hicks indictments, citizen complaints were beginning to mount against various officers with the Special Operations Section, or SOS. SOS was part of the obliquely named Bureau of Operational Services, then the Bureau of Strategic Deployment. Part of the time-tested strategy of those who abuse power or pervert the political process is to give innocuous-sounding names to the organizations they form to use as tools for their surreptitious influence agendas. Law enforcement especially loves the word "Special." SOS was based in Homan Square, a straight shot west of the Loop on the Eisenhower and just south of Garfield Park, but they had operational authority all over the city. They were intended to be an even more aggressive anti-gang, narcotics, and guns unit than the tactical squads that are based in every district.

Public records and news reports say that the first internal investigation concerning the SOS unit happened in 2004, but it was a case in 2005 that stands out as a major red flag for anyone who might be looking. The Melesio family alleged that SOS officers including Jerome Finnigan had stopped their eighteen-year-old son Miguel on the street without any probable cause, took his keys, and made a warrantless entry into the family home, where they stole $13,000 in cash. Miguel was never charged with any crime, and when the family filed an abuse complaint with the police review agency, Finnigan boasted that he was able to shut it down without any findings of impropriety just by placing a single phone call to the right supervisor.

The criminal element within the SOS acted like marauders. They would stop their targets with guns drawn, cuff and search them, take keys and access cards to homes, offices, vehicles, storage lockers, garages . . . basically any place they thought they could find money, drugs, or guns. In one traffic stop alone, Finnigan claimed that they took the driver back to his home and searched it, finding bricks of cash totaling $450,000, which were immediately stolen and divided among three officers. After an almost decade-long campaign of robbing drug dealers and ordinary citizens, abducting people off the streets to rob them, and even a plot to hire hitmen to murder officers who were going to break the code of silence and testify against Finnigan and several others, four SOS officers were charged in federal court and seven in state court, although not all of them were ultimately convicted.

Before his trial, Finnigan decided that several other officers would be strong enough witnesses that they were worth killing. He broached the issue with his fellow SOS officer and indicted co-defendant Keith Herrera, who subsequently wore a wire for the FBI. According to Herrera, Finnigan called it "a paint job," saying he had "some really good painters," and that the job would be done so well that "we'd never have to paint again." Herrera also gave an interview to national media during which he described the specifics of what the SOS squads were doing. He claimed that SOS's standing orders were to get guns and drugs off the street "No matter what. At any cost. Just get 'em off." Those orders were generally understood by tactical officers to be a message from the brass that the ends justified the means. Herrera stated: "Policing the way we did it, there were just certain steps that you had to take. We're dealing with convicted felons, we're dealing with bad people, we're dealing with drug dealers. If you want these people to go to jail, you have to cross the line sometimes. 'Creative writing' was a certain term that bosses used to make sure that the job got done. I didn't just pick up a pen and just learn how to do this. Bosses. Guys that I work with that were older than I was. That had time on the job, you learn this stuff. It's taught to you. 'This is how it's done. This isn't right. Put this in there.' And you gotta listen to them."

In his plea admissions, Finnigan stipulated that he conducted illegal street stops and searches, had arrested and charged people based on false evidence, manipulated narratives in his reports, and fabricated outright lies. After he was sentenced and began serving his term, he granted interviews in which he stated that his crew committed far more crimes than were known or charged, and alleged that he personally knew of nineteen other officers who committed robberies during SOS raids, all with the knowledge and permission of commanding officers at the highest levels of the Chicago Police Department. His admissions and claims were not received well by the department at large, which issued terse denials. However, as for the impact of the SOS activities on the cases they brought to criminal court, prosecutors ended up dismissing approximately 150 cases that the indicted officers had built. Unfortunately for the people who were indicted in those cases, the dismissals only occurred after they were all put through the system to varying degrees, whether to the stage of arrest, indictment, trial, or punishment. In reaction to the PR fallout, the city disbanded the entire Special Operations Section in 2007.

Disbanding SOS was just cosmetic; many other "bosses" and "older guys" were still circulating, teaching, directly and indirectly linking each of these departmentally enabled criminal enterprises and allowing them to sprout and fester like an untreated infection. Robbing drug dealers and forcing them to pay protection tax was obviously not department policy, but failing to stop it obviously was. According to a lawsuit brought by cops who alleged retaliation for reporting corruption, the top brass preferred to bury complaints and project a cleaner image, even if false, rather than continuing the chain of drug-robbery scandals from Austin to Gresham to Miedzianowski to Hicks to SOS, all of which occurred at the same time that the State of Illinois was being relentlessly exposed as systemically sentencing innocent men to death, many of whose cases came from Chicago and brought to light the decades-long torture scheme led by Detective Commander Jon Burge. They allege that is why, despite complaints starting in 1999, the last tactical squad drug robbers who were convicted for crimes they committed during my time in the PD's Office weren't stopped until 2012.

Sergeant Ronald Watts and his partner Officer Kallatt Mohammed were convicted in 2013 in connection with running an extortion racket for over a decade that was centered on the Ida B. Wells

Homes, which were the cluster of housing projects just southeast of the IIT campus and Comiskey Park. They also robbed people, known as "hitting a lick" in street terms, in the Harold L. Ickes Homes and in Stateway Gardens, locations where they imposed protection tax on the dope line that was named after President Obama, requiring dealers to pay them up to $5,000 per week to allow their operations. This earned Watts the nickname "Thirsty Bird." Federal and state prosecutors who were part of the sting that took them down—Operation Brass Tax—concede the fact that Watts and Mohammed, along with approximately a dozen other officers, planted contraband and put false cases on at least dozens, possibly hundreds of people, all while running their own gun and drug sales enterprise.

It also just so happens that two of Watts's and Mohammed's targets ended up being murdered; one was Wilbert "Big Shorty" Moore, who cooperated with the ATF against Watts and was shot dead in 2006. Although members of a street gang called the Hobos were convicted in federal court for that shooting, Watts invoked his constitutional right to remain silent when he was questioned under oath if he had killed, solicited to kill, participated in a conspiracy to kill, or had knowledge of the plan to kill Moore. The second was Kamane "Insane" Fears. According to statements given to police by Fears's girlfriend, she had personally witnessed dozens of payoffs between Fears and Watts. A particularly detailed recollection was of Watts telling Fears that "Easter's coming up, where's my money? My kids need Easter baskets." When Fears told Watts he was refusing further payments and was thinking about cooperating with the feds, he got a call early one morning to go outside his apartment to "handle some business" and ended up being shot seventeen times at close range. The girlfriend heard the shots and looked out the window, and she saw a man in a hoodie walking away. Police determined that the shooter was professional enough to take both cell phones off Fears's body and to pick up all the shell casings on the sidewalk.

Thirsty Bird fed himself so many pockets and pinches that his exploits would eventually lead to the first mass exoneration in Chicago history, and then four more mass exonerations after that, as people fought to at least clear the convictions that had caused them so much damage, even if they couldn't erase their lasting experiential trauma. As of 2020, seventy-five people with a total of ninety-five convictions have been cleared since 2016. A group called the Exoneration Project have posted a timeline of the Watts and Mohammed crimes, with over fifty key events that occurred over more than twenty years. These officers were brazen, violent, lawless, and barely punished, with sentences of approximately two years each for Watts and Mohammed, and the other twelve are still on the force and getting promotions and pensions courtesy of the citizens they victimized. At least prosecutors have put them on an unprecedented "Do Not Call" list that effectively bans them from testifying as State witnesses ever again.

Every PD has had drug cases where the defendant claimed he or she was innocent and the cops were putting the case on them for nothing. Maybe for refusing to snitch, maybe for being in the wrong place at the wrong time. We heard lots of claims that the cops demanded a gun; dozens of times I heard arrestees say that the cops told them they would let them go if they got them a gun, but if not, they were getting a rock. We would try to corroborate what we heard by going out to the scene of the arrest and trying to find witnesses, and then trying to interview them, assess their credibility, and when something sounded useful and believable, trying to persuade them to come to court and testify. Then we would hear about how difficult it was for some people to come to court because they couldn't get off work or find someone to watch their kids, take hours of public transportation, and risk whatever humiliation the State could dig up or whatever retaliation the cops felt like pursuing once court was over.

Sometimes we would find people who told us they had direct, personal experiences with the kinds of abuses that made headlines in the rare cases of FBI undercover operations and ensuing federal convictions. Women who claimed the cops forced sexual favors in exchange for letting them "cop their fixes" without getting taken in. Bar owners who said they were sick and tired of tactical crews coming into the place to do sweeps and searches and driving out their customers, but were too afraid of various inspections and compliance checks to speak up. One time we found a motel owner on Lincoln Avenue who was so angry about the tactical squads coming in and searching rooms and customers that he kept a log of the unmarked cars that drove into his lot; he had plate numbers, the exact times they arrived and left, his observations of the actions they took while they were there, notes about which officers were more aggressive and threatening, and even his guesses about shifts the cops would take in the near future. We actually got him to come to court, and even though we weren't allowed to introduce the log as evidence, I won two cases off his testimony on behalf of a father and son who each caught PCS cases from warrantless room searches.

We had no greater power than the victims themselves to file complaints with the Office of Professional Standards or the Independent Police Review Authority. I knew from personal experience what usually happens when you file a complaint with the watchdog about some police abuse. One night, two friends and I were driving back to the city from a Kane County Cougars game when we came upon a tollbooth on the interstate. As I leaned out to throw my quarters in the basket, a state trooper jumped out from behind the machine and scared me half to death. I was plenty shocked, but I knew I'd paid correctly, so I drove off without hearing if he said anything. We weren't more than a half mile away from the booth when I saw a cruiser racing up behind me. He pulled up even with my window, looked me straight in the eye, then dropped behind me to hit his lights and pull me over. By the time he walked up to my window, a second patrol car and trooper were on the scene as well. The two of them proceeded to tell us that they had seen us drinking cans of beer when we passed through the toll and that we had better give up the cans unless we wanted severe trouble. We had no idea what they were talking about; there was one plastic bottle of diet Sprite that my friend in the back had on the floor, but nobody was drinking any alcohol. We had no cans, no beers, and we were trying to explain all of it very politely and calmly. They decided to try the good cop/bad cop routine on us, with one saying he could help us if we cooperated, and the other absolutely berating us at the top of his lungs while we were standing less than spitting distance from his gaping yap. I clearly remember the bad cop screaming that he was going to search every foot of highway between the tollbooth and where we stopped, and if he found a single beer can, he was going to put his boot in my mouth. Long after we were let go without any charges, I tried to complain to the Illinois State Police. They said they'd look into it and get back to me. Sure enough, despite many friends and associates telling me not to hold my breath, within about a week of my initial complaint, they called me back. To my shock, they simply said there were not two troopers there that night, there was only one, and he conducted himself entirely professionally. I protested that we had three witnesses, and they told me flat-out not to pursue it any further.

Another time I had a client whose son was a high-ranking gang member who was probably involved in interstate car thefts. During a joint FBI and CPD search of their home, several thousand dollars in cash went missing. I called the Chicago FBI field office and reported it on her behalf and was told that if we really wanted it all investigated, the FBI would also perform a thorough investigation into the source of any funds and the legality of how they were earned. The implicit threat was very clear, and we backed off. Other clients had keys taken from them and were afraid that the cops would use them to enter their homes whenever they felt like it. There were many creative ways the cops could leverage pressure on people when they felt motivated to do so. I tried so desperately to understand the motives of the police, to discern any pattern or logic in the behavior I was hearing about and seeing, but the avalanche of conflicting information becomes dizzying; I could not do it. I finally realized that the people who refused to believe stories of police misconduct were not trying to be objective—they had simply chosen sides and dug in. I surrendered in my efforts to persuade and decided to focus instead on spreading my clients' stories to as many people as would listen.

So here's another one: Humid summer evenings in Chicago bring people to their porches. The corollary of the rule that crime goes down in the rain and the snow is that crime goes way, way up in the heat.

In the midst of one sticky city twilight, a pair of teenage Hispanic siblings, brother and sister, took relief on the front stoop of their building while their parents went to the grocery store. What caught their attention was a gangbanger on his bicycle, making circles on the streets immediately adjacent to their block, and looking like he was canvassing pedestrians for *something*. They were not new to the city and not ignorant of the gang activity in their neighborhood, but the brother had recently visited a Marine Corps recruiter as part of making plans for after graduation, and his little sister was an honor student who had kept the right friends and influences as she navigated her high school years. She told me they were discussing whether it was worth it or not to stay outside when the biker shouted his set and pulled his burner from his waistband.

A burst of shots rang out in quick succession, aimed at someone who had been walking on the sidewalk on the opposite side of the street, and giving the siblings time to run for cover back inside. Rounding the corner of the entryway into the living room, they could see through the window as the target ran for his life, darting between parked cars to cross the traffic, and dashing down the path between their house and the one next door (in Chicago, those narrow paths are ironically called "gangways," a term that has nothing to do with fleeing felons but derives from older European and Slavic words for passageway or hallway). Behind the rows of low-rise two-flats and bungalows that are the prevalent residences of the city, Chicago is lined with alleys that are intended to ease garbage collection and facilitate private parking, but they function as great escape routes too. The bike-riding shooter raced off in the other direction, possibly to circle around and try again. Anyone who has lived in an area with gang activity knows that one shooting is likely to be followed by another, as revenge is sought and territory is disputed. The siblings shut the windows and turned off the lights, staying low and listening for clues to the developing situation. They were fully immersed in the pulse of adrenaline and the eerie silence that immediately follows a sudden burst of urban warfare.

They estimated that it took the police a slightly longer time to arrive than usual—around five minutes before the first car was there, and around ten for the rest of the cavalry to show up. They watched pensively as the dusk of evening grew darker, sharpening the contrast between the strobing squad blues and probing flashlight whites. It's not best for your health to be seen talking to the police after an incident like that, so neither of them ventured out to offer whatever detail they might've been able to contribute to the unfolding investigation. People were speaking to the officers and pointing in the direction of their building, but they understood that to be reports about the escape route taken by the fleeing victim.

Soon enough a group of approximately eight to ten officers encircled the ground level of the siblings' home, with three pounding on the front door with a strength and intensity that achieved its intended effect of scaring them into thinking it would be broken down if they didn't respond. Brother and sister had remained close together throughout the whole ordeal up to then, and were within arm's reach of each other when the brother opened the door. That's why she was able to tell me that she was about two feet away with an unobstructed view when the lead officer threw a packet of cocaine at her brother's feet and immediately used it as a pretext to drag him outside and order the other officers to tear the house apart in a search.

In the inevitable confusion, excitement, and shock that surrounds events like a shooting, witnesses report all kinds of things: some accurate, some almost correct but not quite, some just plain wrong, and some that are simply impossible but that our brains just invent as presumptions to piece together what we've seen and turn it into something we understand. Eyewitness testimony is generally horribly unreliable, but ironically has been the backbone of the American criminal justice system since its inception. The results of scientific studies of human witness perceptions, accuracy, and ability to recall would be funny if they weren't so tragic. One of the witnesses on the street reported to police that the shooter ran into my client's house, and the cops were intent on finding the perp and taking a gun off the street. Planted drugs serve as a pretext for both a search and an arrest, and are intended to pressure the thinking of the defendant. The message is that the police have total authority, that the truth is what they say it is, so that even the boundaries of reality cannot save you from whatever they want to do to you. Your only choice is to give them what they demand.

I saw the pictures of the ransacked house. The intensity of the violation of that sanctity and privacy is difficult to describe; police enter wherever they want, take whatever they want, break whatever they want, disrupt the order of everything personal and intimate. They found no bullets or casings, no gun, no gang insignia, no gunshot residue on the siblings' hands, no bicycle, and no additional cocaine or drug paraphernalia—except for a small amount of weed in the brother's sock drawer. They took him on charges for both the coke and the weed, which would be a very effective way to undercut his future ability to file any complaints about the search and arrest. They were not kind to the sister, either, keeping her cuffed and surrounded for the duration of the search of the house, threatening her with various charges of her own, and refusing to tell her where they were taking her brother or what charges they intended to file against him.

In order to believe the drug charges that the police and State ultimately brought against him, you have to believe that he witnessed a shooting and approximately ten minutes of intense police activity right outside his window, and when a significant force of officers announced their office and ordered him to open up, knowing that it was the Chicago Police at his door, he decided to bring the only felony-level contraband in the house with him to the encounter, keep it in his hand rather than hide it anywhere, open the door with his other hand, and then drop the drugs at his own feet, thereby allowing the police to immediately arrest him and instantly obviating their need to get a warrant to search the house. In case anyone was wondering why they went to his house in the first place for this miraculous drug arrest, they carefully documented every aspect of the shooting and allegations of the single witness in their voluminous reports. It was the lightning strike of drop cases, that one-in-a-million luck that granted them instant access to the one place they desperately wanted.

And yet, they weren't the slightest bit embarrassed or reticent to submit this case and their narrative claims of how it unfolded to the courts of Cook County, where they know their word is sacrosanct, and no matter how tall and wild their lies, their word is accepted with near impunity. A felony drug charge follows a person for their entire lives, let alone a felony conviction, and they pursued it. The officers are sworn to an oath that is intended to be sacred, and yet some of them piss all over it without a shred of second thought or hesitation.

On the first court date for the brother, with a prosecutor and judge I did not know well at all, the State offered to give him State's Attorney's Drug School, which is a program of classes about the dangers of controlled substances, and upon the successful completion of which, the charges get dropped and the defendant keeps his record clean. The catch is that each defendant has to sign a stipulated agreement that there is enough evidence to convict them if the case were to proceed to trial. I initially rejected it, telling the ASA that I would advise my client not to sign the stipulation since this case was so egregious that it needed to be aired through testimony. The prosecutor was furious at me, snarling in a way I only saw a handful of times in my career. Defense attorneys are obligated to tell our clients about all plea offers and let them decide, so he and I had that conversation. We would be giving up a guaranteed win (in the form of a clean record) for the chance to argue that my client had some of the drugs, but not all of them. It was a huge risk and a case in point that we need to seek the best result, not the noble fight. In the end I had to go back to the ASA and beg for the school diversion. She told me no—I had offended her so badly that now we needed to suffer the consequences. She let me twist for about fifteen minutes and then relented. The sly smirk on the officer's face as he left court made it all that much harder to swallow.

I had clients sentenced to decades in prison, and I stood next to them while their sentences were pronounced and their lives were effectively ruined. I assisted with cases where people were facing the death penalty and was in the room when execution was presented as a real possibility. I was present for every possible aspect of people's arrests, charges, trials, incarceration, and loss of property and freedom. All of that notwithstanding, I never saw anyone more emotionally traumatized than the sister was; the breathless way she tried to describe what the police had done to her and her brother through her choking tears, stinted speech, agonal gasps, trembling convulsions, and searing pain is something that will stay with me for the rest of my days.

X. DEATH

Chicago's central jail has been located at 26th and California since 1871. Officially named the Chicago House of Correction when it opened, people called it the "Bridewell," an antiquated architectural term used to describe public buildings with dimensions and parapets reminiscent of a particular castle that belonged to King Henry VII near St. Bride's Well in London. Maybe our Bridewell had more in common with the Tower of London; between 1871 and 1962, more than 150 executions by hanging and electrocution occurred in and around the building that became Division 1 of the Cook County Jail. Hangings took place outdoors in an inner courtyard of the complex, but the electric chair was bolted to the floor of one of the concrete chambers in the basement.

From the outside, the building designated as Division 1 certainly looked like it was standing there for over a century. Inside there were numerous "upgrades" that allowed it to remain in daily use as one of the maximum-security divisions, but it still looked and smelled medieval on the inside too. All visitors entered through a single main entrance that was built with the solemn grandeur of important civic structures of the time, but that became run-down and neglected in reflection of the minimalist brutality of the modern standard. There were no dedicated attorney-client visiting facilities there; we just got put into whatever space was available in one of the common rooms in the basement, regardless of the deck where our clients were housed. After passing through security in the entrance hall, lawyers were taken down to the basement in an elevator that was small, usually overcrowded, and closed with a second set of doors that resembled jail bars. There was no light except fluorescent, and there was no air except stale must.

Arriving at the bottom floor, sets of deputies shouted announcements to each other for safe passage down the corridors while the inmates stood fast behind a yellow line painted on the floor about a foot from the wall. As a younger PD conducting client visits in Division 1, some of the deputies loved to tease that they were going to put me in the old death chamber for my meetings, and wasn't it a shame that the chair couldn't still be there to be used on defense attorneys and their clients together. The jokers were usually the biggest slobs on the deck, the ones who looked like they were about one more meatball sandwich away from a four-alarm grabber, but they thought they were hilarious and I understood their misery. I was never sure if I was in the actual death chamber or not, but the whole building was a miserable labyrinth of stone and crushing confinement with the sense of the Grim Reaper's antechamber. Then again, I've never been in a jail or prison that didn't feel that way.

Working in the criminal justice system in a death penalty state gave me extensive exposure to murder cases and death penalty litigation. In addition to the opportunities to work on those cases as my experience developed, I was trained and mentored as a trial attorney by veterans of the Public Defender's Office Homicide Task Force. They're the group of lawyers whose experience, skill, and dedication get perversely rewarded by assigning them exclusively to the most high-stakes, stressful, and depressing cases that the entire system can throw at them. They are considered the elite of the PD's Office, implying that ambitious attorneys should aspire to their ranks, but honestly their work terrified me. There were plenty of formal and informal messages about managing the stresses of our jobs in general, and it was impossible to escape the persistent rumors about the kinds of personal damages being suffered by those who take all the blows of being the most reviled rung of the criminal justice system and whose all-murder caseload consists of abject darkness piled like cord.

As rare as it was for me to meet people who had direct experience with the death penalty, it was rarer still to meet people who had no opinion about it. Following disclosure of a career as a criminal defense attorney, right after the "How can you do that?" question, hypotheticals about representing killers and child molesters are never far behind. Regardless of the basis of their opinions, people can easily compensate for lack of experience or expertise with feelings. When it's an abstract question, it seems like there's no shortage of hot takes.

For authentic understanding, anyone should be grateful not to know the anguish my former PD colleague Jeanne Bishop has to live with for the rest of her life. When I was in high school in 1990, a kid who was about the same age as I was decided to commit a thrill killing, just to see how it felt. He lived in Winnetka and attended New Trier, arguably the most prestigious public high school in our area, just a few miles to the north of mine. Rather than enjoying the benefits of his family and educational opportunities, he indulged the cruelest of his curiosities and picked a house across the street from the local police station, which he later admitted was a twisted attempt at taunting the law. The house he chose belonged to Jeanne's sister and brother-in-law, Nancy and Richard Langert. They were in their mid-twenties, part of a large and loving extended family, expecting their first child, and looking forward to what should have been a beautiful and successful life ahead.

Instead, this sadistic kid invaded their home, held them at gunpoint while he tied them up, and dragged them downstairs into their basement. Once there, the killer wasted no time on his mission, using his .357 Magnum to execute Richard with a point-blank shot to the back of his head as Nancy looked on. Immediately turning to Nancy and her unborn child, he began to taunt her. Backed into the corner of her basement and having just been forced to witness the murder of her husband, she begged the teenaged killer to spare the life of her baby, and clasped her arms to shield the growing child inside her. To ensure her maximum suffering, the gunman shot Nancy three times in the abdomen. A deputy Cook County medical examiner testified at the subsequent trial that the bullets effectively exploded the fetus to the point that there was no way to discern its gender, and that Nancy was most likely alive for fifteen minutes after she was shot. As she lay dying, she dragged herself beside her dead husband and used her own blood to draw a heart and the letter "u" on the wall as her final message of love and goodbye to her family.

Nancy's older sister Jeanne graduated from Northwestern Law School, forged a successful legal career for herself in private practice, and married a man who was the talent agent for internationally renowned jazz pianist Dave Brubeck. She probably didn't need to work at all, and she certainly didn't have to choose a second act of her career as a public defender, but she did. She also became a tireless advocate against the death penalty and in favor of rehabilitative justice in general, saying, "Our loved ones are not honored by mercilessly throwing a young person's life away." Anyone can agree or disagree with her, but nobody can say that she doesn't know what she's talking about, and few people can speak to the subject with the kind of deep personal understanding for which she paid such an unimaginable price.

Illinois has a troubled history with the death penalty. By 1999 a series of events that produced concrete proof of systemic police lies forced the State of Illinois to draw a line where municipalities and counties could or would not: Governor George Ryan decided it was finally time to stop condemning innocent men, many of whom had been framed by the police. The first domino to fall in the momentum toward that decision was the acceptance of DNA evidence, irrefutably establishing the innocence of various convicts of rape and murder. Of course, initial efforts by defense attorneys to have evidence retested and defendants retried was met with furious obstinance by prosecutors and judges around the state whose reelection funds live and die on police union donations, but the dam was cracking.

The first three exonerations off Illinois's Death Row occurred in the mid-'80s and early '90s and were actually convictions that had been based on civilian perjury—just straight-up lies by witnesses who were protecting their self-interests or the interests of their friends and lovers at the easy and simple cost of someone else's life. But the strength of DNA evidence demanded respect that flip-flopping witnesses never did, and a sort of revolution occurred. Cases that redefined standards about the strength of evidence had similar impacts in their sentencing implications too. The 1995 Nicarico case in DuPage County just outside of Chicago exploded onto the national scene with the revelations that Rolando Cruz and Alejandro Hernandez were innocent (covered in more detail in chapter 5), but had nonetheless been sent to Death Row based on a conspiracy among three prosecutors and four sheriff's deputies who became known as the "DuPage 7" when they themselves were arrested for fabricating confessions that DNA flatly contradicted. The DuPage 7 were subsequently acquitted in a bench trial that was a powerful signal to law-enforcement officers across the state that regardless of the depravity of official misconduct, extremely wide justifications can be found for attempted murder with a badge.

Railroading—the practice of forcing convictions against innocent people and against the weight of the evidence—has a long history around the world, and the United States and Illinois are no exceptions. Whether the DNA revolution carried such weight that its proofs simply could not be ignored, or progress toward greater integrity is a genuine hallmark of our American justice system, at least exonerations were becoming possible to counteract some of the worst injustices. In 1996 the Ford Heights Four from the southern end of Cook County were belatedly exonerated for a double murder they did not commit. Their case failed to capture national attention in the same way that the Nicarico case did, but Willie Rainge, Kenneth Adams, Verneal Jimerson, and Dennis Williams spent decades in prison (with Jimerson and Williams under the sentence of death) before DNA retesting and persistent appellate advocacy set them free. Two additional exonerations, of Gary Gauger and Carl Lawson, from Illinois's Death Row occurred during the same year that the two condemned men from the Ford Heights Four were released; Gauger's conviction rested on a fabricated confession, and Lawson's case had a strikingly weak bit of forensic evidence that went unchallenged in part because of an outrageous conflict of interest that saw the defendant represented at trial by the same prosecutor who had arraigned him. Although there was a very disturbing pattern of fabricated confessions, false testimony, and procedural flaws leading to death sentences, a new pattern was beginning to emerge in Illinois of trying to remedy egregious injustices, even if some of the damage could never be undone, and even if the process was agonizingly slow and difficult.

The next three salvations off Death Row had been arrested and convicted in Chicago, and they each gained their release in 1999. Steven Smith was the first. His murder conviction had been primarily based on the testimony of a crackhead whose boyfriend was an alternative suspect, but the victim was a law-enforcement officer and there was intense pressure to hold someone accountable. The second was Ronald Jones, who was convicted of murder on the strength of a confession that he claimed the Chicago Police had beaten out of him. There was no physical evidence that linked him to the crime; however, there was semen that the judge and State refused to have tested for DNA, even though it was introduced as evidence by the State for the purpose of proving that Jones's alleged confession was genuine. When the testing was ultimately ordered by the appellate court in post-conviction relief, Jones was excluded as the source and proven innocent. Nobody went back and investigated how his "confession" was obtained or why it was judged constitutionally sound enough to be used.

Anthony Porter was the third. His case got massive media attention because it was taken on as a joint project by the Northwestern School of Law's Legal Clinic and the university's School of Journalism. Porter was just hours away from his execution when he won a stay from the Illinois Supreme Court based on concerns that his IQ was too low for him to comprehend the final punishment he was facing. The stay disregarded claims that he was actually innocent, as he had maintained throughout his sixteen years on Death Row. His last-minute reprieve bought enough time for Northwestern's investigators to expose fundamental flaws in the original case against him and cast serious doubt on his guilt. His conviction for double murder had been built on eyewitness testimony, but the reinvestigation found new witnesses on Porter's behalf and revealed that a crucial witness against Porter claimed his original testimony was false and had been coerced by police abuse. Most dramatically, the Northwestern reinvestigation found a totally different suspect who was persuaded to walk into a police station in Milwaukee and gave a videotaped confession to having been the actual killer back in 1982. Ironically, that confession was the one in relation to those murders that the State considered suspicious and possibly coerced. Officially, the State considers those murders unsolved. Regardless, prosecutors finally dropped the charges against Porter and set him free. Between the time that the death penalty was reinstated in the 1970s after briefly being ruled unconstitutional by the US Supreme Court and the time that Governor Ryan announced his moratorium on its use throughout our state, *Illinois had more condemned inmates exonerated than executed*, with a macabre scorecard of 13–12.

Maybe those numbers were not just the mathematical tipping point but the political one, too, becoming the final straw that shattered whatever fragile faith had existed in the reliability of the death penalty in Illinois and, by extension, exposed fundamental flaws and the desperate need for reform in our criminal justice system overall. After all, executions were supposed to be the most solemn duty of the State and were presumed to be the responsibility for which all involved parties had the greatest reverence. It had to be asked that if that process could be so callously abused, what other supposedly sacrosanct limits were being discarded in the name of expediency? Or worse, being sacrificed to the avarice of authoritarianism or racism? Speculation into the precise reason for Governor Ryan's altruistic mercy has included possible motivation based on DNA testing advances, the collective score of exonerations, or maybe a particular case among them that produced a shock, revulsion, and tsunami of bad PR that was just too much to take (with the two favorites in the last category being Cruz and Porter). Less commonly considered for attribution is the possibility that behind the headlines, Ryan feared an exposé was coming that was going to make things a lot worse.

Worse than deadly mistakes is murderous persecution, and that was Jon Burge. Burge was a sworn member of the Chicago Police Department for over twenty years, rising from patrolman to detective in Area 2 Robbery, then commander of Area 2 violent crimes, then commander of the bomb and arson unit, and finally to detective commander of Area 3. He was brass; his policies were department practices because they came from him. And his policies for over twenty years included torturing suspects to coerce confessions using his "Midnight Crew" detective squad and their techniques of beating people with steel flashlights, cuffing detainees to walls and other stationary objects for days at a time, mock executions, shoving guns in suspects' mouths, burns, electric shocks with a cattle prod and a battery box that was allegedly identical to a device that was used in Vietnam when Burge was an army MP there, Russian roulette, holding guns to the heads of interrogees' children, shooting their pets, and the Burge special: suffocation by placing plastic typewriter covers over suspects' heads and choking them into submission. The exact number of victims and the exact methods used on each one were extremely difficult to prove, but an internal report written in 1990 by the CPD Office of Professional Standards—called the Goldston Report—listed fifty separate incidents that were deemed credible. The Goldston Report characterized Burge's abuses as "methodical" and "systematic." Further investigations found at least 125 victims, with investigative journalists from the *Chicago Reader*, the *Guardian*, and the *Intercept* variously reporting that there had been many more, possibly over two hundred.

Several federal investigations occurred and at least two special prosecutors were appointed to try to expose everything Burge had done and bring him to justice, but by the time there was any political will to address these abuses in depth, the statute of limitations had run out on the most appropriate charges for virtually all of the provable acts of torture. It was conveniently too late to prosecute Burge's worst crimes. However, Burge was prosecuted and sent to prison for obstruction of justice and perjury related to his denials of committing these atrocities during civil depositions in some of the litany of lawsuits against him. Federal Judge Milton Shadur called it "common knowledge" that Burge and "many" detectives he supervised had used torture as a routine technique for years. The city paid out over $175 million in lawsuit settlements, defense fees, and reparations related to his activities. Before he could be stopped, Burge and his cohorts sent ten men to Death Row, all of whom were still seeking review of their convictions at the time the world learned that Illinois was better at sentencing innocent men to death than we were at executing guilty ones. It seems quite possible that at the time he took action in 1999, Governor Ryan knew there would be more embarrassing revelations about how Illinois stocked the waiting line for our execution chamber. Sure enough, between 2003 and 2009, five of the Burge ten were exonerated, leaving Detective Commander Jon Burge and his Midnight Crew responsible for a quarter of the innocent men sentenced to death in Illinois.

Every single time some episode of grotesque injustice is brought to light, there is a chorus of voices eager to paint the calamity as rare, unique, past, over, closed, and incapable of reoccurrence. These strike me as the same type of people who religiously dispute the phenomenon of evolution and its applicability to our social and political behavior, or wannabe revisionist historians who thrive in the darkness of public ignorance. As much as we may wish that Burge's depravity was unique, his legacy was passed directly to Detective Reynaldo Guevara, who has been accused of framing at least 52 people for murders they did not commit. Among those 52 allegations, as of 2020, 20 have been exonerated, 14 remain in prison, 16 have completed their sentences but still have convictions on their records, and 2 died while incarcerated. Guevara's false convictions were accomplished by a mix of actions that the Illinois Appellate Court described as "alarming acts of misconduct," including beatings, coerced confessions, and manipulated lineups that produced false identifications. Guevara was working both sides of the conviction business according to the FBI, who wrote in their 2001 report in the Miedzianowski investigation that Guevara accepted tens of thousands of dollars in bribes as part of a kickback scheme with at least one private defense attorney to make murder cases "go away." Not just murders but, according to the same FBI report, Guevara ran a racket in the Humboldt Park neighborhood by arresting people on gun and drug cases and then allowing them to "buy their way out of trouble." Apparently his schemes were at least partly in response to massive personal financial pressures that included alimony obligations from a divorce, approximately half a million dollars in medical debt, and wage garnishments for court-ordered child support for the numerous children he's fathered out of wedlock—the exact number of which he has claimed not to know but has estimated to be "about fifteen."

Guevara managed to become a detective in 1990, despite not passing the requisite written exam, and retired with a full pension in 2005. He has numerous documented complaints against him for his use of racial slurs, including calling a woman he assaulted a "silly nigga bitch" and a man whom he attacked in a road rage incident a "nigger dog." Various lawsuits against him for civil rights violations have been successful for the plaintiffs to the tune of tens of millions of dollars, despite his continuous efforts to scuttle all claims against him by invoking his constitutional right not to incriminate himself, the most famous example of which was his performance in federal court in 2018 during which he asserted his Fifth Amendment right to remain silent more than two hundred times, including when directly asked if he had ever framed anyone for crimes they did not commit. The jury in that case also found that the Chicago Police Department was guilty of systemic unconstitutional policies that tolerated and encouraged official misconduct. Mounting exonerations and verdicts finally made it impossible for the State's Attorney's Office to ignore the overwhelming number of claims against Guevara, leading to a comprehensive review of his work by the SAO's Conviction Integrity Unit. Dating back to the 1980s, more than seventy false convictions of the innocent have been proven and exposed against the Chicago Police Department, with each of the Miedzianowski, Burge, and Guevara scandals being described in the media as among the most significant policing scandals in US history and earning Chicago the unofficial reputation as "false conviction capital of the United States."

Nobody knows that better than the men and women of the Cook County Public Defender's Office.

It's our exact job, professional duty, and moral obligation to prevent false convictions. To that end, we work to prevent every conviction that we can. We aren't supposed to be the only governmental entity with the solemn responsibility to prevent false convictions, but it does feel that way most of the time because of the working relationship between the State and the police. The interaction between the offices and agencies at each Cook County courthouse creates a dynamic that's pretty consistent throughout all the branches, even though individual personalities form a cast of characters that makes each place unique. There's an unstated but clearly understood hierarchy that's defined by whose ass you have to kiss to get your job done the best you can: at the top of the chain are the judges, then the state's attorneys, then the sheriffs, then the clerks, then the Probation Department, and then us.

Probably within each office, but definitely in ours, there is an esprit de corps that follows the leadership of the chief and deputy supervisor. In order to keep an eye on everything that's going on in all the courtrooms, the bosses don't have courtroom assignments like the line assistants do. For the most part, the bosses' litigating days are over, which means their personalities aren't defined by the adversarial fighting anymore. Having risen above the fray, they tend to relax. For whatever reason, some people never make it to management, and they form a layer of topped-out, system-savvy grit that just keeps grinding, eating shit sandwiches, and dropping truth bombs as they mark off their days left until retirement on those Clerk's Office calendars that are printed and distributed like wallpaper at every courthouse each year. Obviously, we lose the most, and whether that's right or wrong in the big picture, it takes some getting used to. There are PDs who are generally resigned to that reality and roll with it, and then there are PDs who fight against it and burn off energy like a sparkler. Sometimes it feels like fighting against gravity. The key is choosing your battles, having thick skin, and protecting your credibility and reputation at all costs.

There's not the slightest doubt which side is favored by politics; at any given time, Illinois has more than 750 police agencies in operation, many of which are concentrated around Chicago with overlapping jurisdictions. A person who is standing in Chicago is being simultaneously "served and protected" by the Chicago Police, Illinois State Police, Cook County Sheriff's Police, Cook County Sheriff's Office Department of Court Services, Cook County Forest Preserve Police, Illinois Secretary of State Police, University of Illinois Police,

University of Chicago Police, Northwestern University Police, Metra Police, Burlington Northern and Santa Fe Railway Police, Metropolitan Water Reclamation District Police, the State's Attorney's Investigation Bureau, and all of the municipal departments of the cities and villages that border the city. The redundancy of so many layers of police forces makes no sense, except as the golden goose of patronage jobs that are so valuable because of Illinois's unique and bizarre state constitution that has an amendment enshrining permanent corruption by making it illegal to take away benefits from government employees after such benefits have been conferred. Sealing the job security of all those cops, regardless of misconduct or liability, are layers of unions to represent each rank within the department such as patrolman, sergeants, detectives, and lieutenants. For all the thousands of times I've heard the Fraternal Order of Police and politicians mention the morale of the police and how crucially their feelings should be factored into regulatory, budgetary, and reform considerations, I've never heard a single comment or concern for the morale of the public defenders. It's really weird and depressing to be the agency that most people want to see fail and to be constantly politically sabotaged and handicapped, even though our role is set out in the US Constitution and is the implementation of the highest virtues of American justice.

Politics can be abstract, but at least part of the reason for the disparity in treatment between cops and everybody else isn't abstract at all: it's death. The police are specifically required to face deadly danger, and the streets of Chicago certainly provide endless horrific opportunities for death to come calling for first responders. Even though defense lawyers and police officers are cast in the role of adversaries by the necessities of the American pursuit of justice, and even though those of us on the defense see the worst of humanity on both sides of the law, as we sit around our desks and conference tables and com-

miserate about our shared despair, we really do take the time to respect the fact that society is much better off with—and even depends
on—those few souls who are brave enough to run toward the danger.
We understand that it takes a distinct mettle to hear the call of duty
and respond. We know that we, too, might need to call 911 at some
point in the face of grave harm, and that the individuals who respond
to those calls just might be the difference between life and death.

In terms of danger on the job, my worst brush with a rampaging
defendant wasn't that bad, and it just so happened to occur when I
was with an officer I knew as a father figure. I had the distinct plea-
sure of working with a sheriff's deputy who was a retired Skokie Police officer, and he had been my "Officer Friendly" when I was in
first grade. On one of those infrequent but oddly regular days at the
courthouse when anger grips the soul of someone at the very end of
their emotional rope and a burst of desperation turns physical, this
deputy stood between me and a detainee who was charging through
the lockup next to my courtroom on his way to a wild escape attempt. He'd already managed to knock over several other deputies
in the lockup and get into the courtroom, from where his plan was
apparently just to run out into the hallway and see where he could go
from there. He wasn't armed, and it wasn't anywhere near the level
of danger that officers confront in active shooter situations, but the
guy certainly didn't care how many people he had to harm, or how
badly, on his way to the exit. He was about six feet away from me
with only Big John Hammond in the way, and if we had been standing just a few feet over from where we were when he burst out of the
lockup, we would have been his next targets. There's a panic button in every courtroom, and when that is used, the rush of urgency
in the flood of law-enforcement officers who come running is truly
breathtaking. An emergency code is broadcast that gets picked up by
multiple agencies, so it's not only the sheriffs who come running—it's
everybody, in a horde, at full sprint. They caught him, and when it all

calmed down, John and I had a chance to reflect on our moment of truth. We hugged, and he said, "Don't worry, buddy, I'd take a bullet for you if I had to." In my heart of hearts, I know he absolutely would.

Other public defenders are far less lucky. We get hired in groups and go through initial training together as a class. One of the people in my starting cluster was Richard Kruss, a man of slender build and bookish features. He had an overall appearance and demeanor of kindness and intellectual curiosity, which is to say that some people could interpret his presence as weak, the sort of person who would be a typical target for bullies who tend to go after those they perceive as easy prey. A few years into our tour of duty, he was standing with his client before the bench in a courtroom at 26th and Cal when apparently a strategy disagreement between them became intolerable to the defendant to the point where he proceeded to punch Rick in the head hard enough to fracture his skull. Probably all the experienced PDs in the Felony Trial Division have had moments where a client is spiraling to the brink, and we rely on the courtroom sheriffs to sense the same things we do and intervene, which they do with powerful purpose. But from what I understand, Rick's client was able to mask his fuming until he struck like a snake and landed his furious blow. As we received updates about his convalescence and held discussions about how to ensure we would be safe in moments of crisis, most of us had the feeling that there are lots of defendants who see us all as someone to blame and would be more than happy to inflict whatever damage they could in aimless acts of revenge against "the system" they hate so viscerally. However, as much as we may have thought "there but for the grace of God go I," it really may have just been something about Rick—eleven years later Rick got stabbed by another client during a jail visit when the guy took out a shiv he'd crudely fashioned from an asthma inhaler. Rick survived, albeit somewhat worse for wear. I hope the word got around about that poor fellow being a lot tougher than he looks, but it would be even nicer if he gets taken care of by Cook County in such a way that ensures he doesn't ever have to worry about something like that happening again. You know what they say about strike three.

Still, we don't dare compare the dangers that we face to that of the police. In the summer of 1998, I had finished two years of internships in the PD's Office and was studying for the bar exam. Soccer was the predominant backdrop for my studies as the World Cup played out in France. Since I still had my student practitioner law license and the courthouse was close to where I lived, I went to the office whenever time allowed in order to keep current on cases and stay attuned to the events that shape courthouse culture. Everything lay ahead for me, and I felt the full crest of youth and promise.

Michael Ceriale must have felt that too. Just a few years older than I was, he a little more than a year into his career as a Chicago Police officer. He must've done well as a probationary officer and with his initial patrol duties because he managed to get detailed to a plainclothes tactical unit fairly quickly, which was a coveted assignment for the officers who wanted action. That was the assignment that drew him to a narcotics surveillance post near Wentworth Gardens on the South Side in the early evening hours of a mid-August summer weekend. It's not hard to imagine how he might've felt as a twenty-six-year-old officer of the law, strapped up with the tools of power in the form of a gun, vest, badge, and an army of reinforcements available at the touch of a radio button, all while believing he was devoting his strength to the forces of good. Whether it was a failure of tactics or just the realities of doing the job, a gang spotter saw him and ordered a child enforcer to fire off a shot from a handgun. In the meticulous investigation that followed, the distance between the shooter and Officer Ceriale was reported as being between sixty and seventy yards, an enormous range for a handgun shot. During the milliseconds that bullet was airborne, there must have been a concurrent universe of micro-actions: environmental elements like wind and humidity, movements of man and machine, synaptic orchestra of impression and deed. The alignment of fate was bitterly cruel; those were not Michael Ceriale's last moments on earth, but they were the last moments of his vitality. The bullet struck him in the gut, just below the line of protection afforded by his ballistic vest. He languished in the hospital for six agonizing days, but ultimately lost his life in the service of the people of the city of Chicago. Compounding the tragedy, the juvenile who did the shooting was sentenced as an adult to sixty years in prison. I can't recall that kid's name, but Officer Ceriale's sentence is eternal, and I will forever remember his.

If you've ever seen the transport of a wounded or deceased officer in Chicago, you can never forget it. A phalanx of countless vehicles, lights ablaze and sirens wailing, with an additional mobile squadron of officers darting out ahead to stop traffic at every intersection and clear the way, sometimes shutting down entire boulevards or highways along miles of routes. Walkways outside the hospital or morgue become thronged with officers and firemen, many stock-still in rigid salute. Frenzied action at the core of the cortege occurs with such concentrated strength that it appears as though the actors believe there might be a chance to stop time itself if enough energy can be focused. They look like they are trying to move heaven and earth to impose their will. On those solemn occasions when they lose their desperate battle, it looks and sounds like they're trying to ensure that the soul of the departed ascends to the great beyond with a fanfare that commands the attention of the saints and angels. If there are any concerns about such a spectacle being too expensive or self-adulatory, they're overcome by certain cultural preferences. Killings of the police are soldiers' deaths; there is heroism in their sacrifice and they want you to see.

Killings by the police, on the other hand, have a different pageantry altogether.

To kill a person in the name of the law is the ultimate use of police power, so it's also the ultimate test of the legitimacy of that power. Something that has always stood out to me, specifically because the police make such a big show of the transport of a wounded officer, is that they don't show anywhere nearly the same urgency for the people they shoot. Behavior is the outward manifestation of inner intent; if the actions are different, the priorities are different. If they aren't there to protect and serve the public with the same intensity and dedication that they protect and serve themselves, especially when someone is dying, then they don't care if the public respects police power, they just want people to fear it. As a test of governmental legitimacy it fails miserably, and it becomes the duty of moral people to work against it.

Whenever the police kill someone in Chicago, public defenders learn about it from the news just like everybody else. The first thing we do—nearly each and every one of us in the Felony Trial Division, anyway—is to check if the deceased was our client, past or present. Even with a roster of tens of thousands of clients, sometimes over many years, certain names leave a permanent residue of familiarity that surfaces with little effort. When death or a particularly heavy penitentiary sentence catches up with a client of yours, you think back on all the meetings, conversations, interactions, and opportunities you had to counsel that person and the effort you put in, trying to figure out if there was something more you could have said or done that might've changed the path that led to such a grim outcome. Most of the time you can't find a single moment that sticks out as an obvious crossroads, or that might have caused permanent damage as an opportunity missed. Rationally, there's probably nothing we did or didn't do that could even be considered a remote—let alone proximate—cause for the disaster that's occurred. Our powerlessness is clear enough on a daily basis; to find absolution in the extension of that notion is not a long walk. But we're all familiar with the butterfly effect theory. The question lingers.

The second thing most of us do is delve into the news coverage to learn as much as we can about what happened. The combination of morbid curiosity and daily immersion in the profession of legal review of police activity leads many of us to pay close attention to major incidents, just to learn whatever we can about the circumstances, the people involved, and the construction of the official narrative that gets offered to the public. Many PDs take the role of public guardians very seriously and want to be as informed and as prepared as possible for the biggest challenges of our careers, whenever they may come. Since one of the major failings of our office is the lack of any centralized system for data collection and analysis to take the massive amount of piecemeal information we have about police tactics and reporting and turn it into actionable impeachment when officers with a history or pattern of provable lies testify on our routine burglaries and drug busts, many of us try to at least understand the mechanics of cover-ups when they surface in the headlines of heater cases.

Nothing has advanced evidence collection more than video cameras. In terms of both concrete proof in specific cases, and in the larger conversation about the realities of certain police-citizen interactions, video has changed our lives. Video recordings provide such an enormous amount of information that they have become a trial lawyer's cliché; arguments about a specific piece of evidence being taken out of context very often use the rhetorical tool of claiming that the judge or jury are being shown a single frame instead of the whole roll of film, and it works because so many people understand the reference. What began with camcorders in the 1980s has become a world full of surveillance cameras, dashcams, Ring cams, smartphones, and bodycams worn by officers themselves. It's a bedrock legal concept that the opportunity to observe is a core component of evidentiary quality, and therefore evidentiary use. What can be objectively seen can be independently judged, and video allows everyone to see so much more than ever before.

Before the Rodney King incident in Los Angeles in 1992, there was very little national conversation, let alone national consensus, about the topic of police brutality. The occurrence of a savage beating by a gaggle of officers who were whaling away with their batons, punches, and kicks on a man who was already down on his knees begging for mercy after a traffic stop wouldn't have created a national shift in thinking about the existence and scale of abuse of power, because things like that already happened many times over, and very few people acknowledged it or even cared. However, the video of that beating being shown on the national news, over and over again, did impact the national consciousness because victims finally had concrete proof and deniers had to watch. There were still many people who didn't want to acknowledge or understand the true scope of the problem, but there were no longer any who hadn't seen it in action. That incident exacted a steep price from their local justice system that the whole country could see too: the O.J. Simpson acquittal a few years later. White people generally understood that verdict as an aberration of spiteful revenge, whereas minorities generally saw it as progress toward a new standard, wherein the reality of police abuses would be factored into assessments of their credibility, and powerful people who were accustomed to winning would have to accept some losses going forward. Either way, the common ground was the agreement that there are steep costs when injustice occurs, and lessons were learned.

Chicago's video breakthrough wasn't just simple police brutality; we've been sort of used to that since the Battle of Michigan Avenue at the 1968 Democratic National Convention, and the local attitude toward the issue is one of natural consequence, perhaps best encapsulated by the millennial expression "fuck around, find out." Our YouTube flashpoint was the murder of Laquan McDonald by Officer Jason Van Dyke, which seemed to capture so much attention based on a combination of pure Chicago factors including the ferocity with which the city resisted initial efforts to release the recording for public viewing, and the stark disparity between the official version of events and what was clearly shown on the video. The release not only laid bare the shooting itself, with its barbarous excess in the "empty the clip" ethos that police training ingrains into deadly confrontations, but also exposed the fabrications in the official attempts to justify the use of deadly force, and the cavalier attitude toward truth that's been created by decades of allowing lies as a matter of routine in Cook County. That video built momentum toward reform by leading to Van Dyke's murder conviction and a 2017 US Department of Justice investigation and report that, once again, excoriated the Chicago Police Department's "culture of excessive violence" and deficiencies in training, oversight, and accountability. Raw footage hasn't been a panacea though. They still killed Harith Augustus and Adam Toledo, among others, and still tried to murder Ariel Roman and Daniel Mares, among others. Prevention of disaster seems like it would require complete disempowerment of the FOP (Fraternal Order of Police) at the very least, and that's out of the question for the foreseeable future. Accountability is political, so except for rare situations where it's expedient, that probably isn't coming anytime soon, either. At least the film and digital memory storage devices are increasingly beyond the reach of the long arm of the law, so the evidence has a chance to speak for itself. That absolutely changes the balance of power in the pursuit of justice, just as fundamentally as DNA did; due to the volume of lenses and instantaneous accessibility of viral viewing, probably far more.

I suppose there will always be some officers who are savvy enough to keep certain things out of the public eye using the privacy offered by vehicles, hospitals, police stations, semi-secret detention centers like Homan Square, and certain dark spots in the streets they know so well. I once had a client who was accused of masturbating in an alley, and he told me that the arresting officers drove him around seemingly aimlessly for forty-five minutes until they stopped in an enclosed lot behind an abandoned building, pulled him out of the car, forced him onto his knees on the ground, and made him lick the words "Chicago Police" on the side of their squad car. He said they were taunting him about being a pervert and told him they were gonna knock his teeth out as a favor so that he could "give better blowjobs to his faggot friends." If he was making it up, it certainly was oddly specific. I checked the reports; the difference in the time on scene and the time they booked him into the lockup at the station was exactly as long as he'd alleged, and far longer than the amount of time a direct route would have required. He was too scared to complain.

Another client was nearly charged with murder as a result of one of the first known incidents where the Chicago Police appeared to have killed someone with a Taser. The client and his partner were involved in some sort of disturbance that was loud enough to get the attention of a neighbor in their apartment building, and the police arrived to find the partner in the hallway, very agitated but only partially dressed. Trying to take control of the scene and understand what was going on, the officers ordered the partner to calm down, or at least stand still. Based on some combination of the partner's inability or unwillingness to regain self-control, and a heightened sense of danger due to the confines of the hallway and the concern that more neighbors could emerge from their apartments at any moment and be caught up in a possibly violent situation, the officers used a Taser on the partner, who promptly dropped dead. Apparently thinking it would be better if they could blame someone else for the death, they immediately arrested my client on the suspicion of murder. They claimed that the partner must have been so agitated as the result of taking drugs that they suspected my client of providing; they further surmised that this imaginary drug use caused an overdose death that, naturally, wasn't at all related to their use of the Taser.

As it happened, this case occurred after I'd left the PD's Office and gone into private practice. The client was a man of sufficient means to have relied on the services of my firm in some capacity other than criminal defense, and while the police were busy with whatever medical checks and creative thinking exercises they'd been moved to by the carcass in the hallway, our client had the sense to call his lawyers for help. The lawyer at our firm with whom he'd established his attorney-client relationship was not normally engaged in this sort of practice, so he assembled a three-man team including myself and sent us racing to the apartment to intervene however we could on the client's behalf.

Arriving at the scene before the police had the chance to take our client away, we explained who we were and the purpose of our presence. Faced with the mutual demand from client and lawyer for immediate consultation, and having just read the man the Miranda warnings that clarified his right to do so, the police allowed one of us to enter their cordon to speak with their arrestee. As I was fresh from years of directly relevant experience as a PD, I was chosen for the task. In what seemed to us to be a deliberate attempt to keep that consultation as short as possible, the police informed us that they'd be transporting the client to the station right that minute. Their joust was instantly parried by the senior lawyer among us three by inform-ing both the police and me that I would be joining the client in the squad car for the ride. Slightly bemused but never at a loss to counter, the police acquiesced, provided I would submit to being searched before getting in. Unarmed, unafraid, and trying to provide the very best level of service at the most critical of junctures, I agreed and was placed in that familiar position on the car and thoroughly searched.

What none of us had noticed until that point was the somewhat large media presence on the scene. They'd arrived following a time-tested ploy of monitoring police radio transmissions and showing up as quickly as possible to capture dramatic images that might boost ratings on nightly broadcasts or bump sales of morning editions. For the benefit of any young lawyers who may be reading this, if your media debut involves images of you being starfished on the trunk of a cop car and then being given one of those signature head dunks by detectives as they guide you into the back seat, while the banner underneath reads something about a suspected overdose homicide in a posh apartment building on the Gold Coast, regardless of the excellence of your intentions, your supervising partner will be *furious*, even if he's the one who sent you there. Apparently, the proper thing to do under such circumstances is to demand that the police search you outside the view of the cameras. Live and learn.

Anyway, if you've never been inside the transport of a murder arrest, allow me to describe: My client was handcuffed; I was not. One detective was driving the car, and a second sat in the front passenger seat, twisted all the way around and facing us the entire time, watching every move and interaction between me and my client. They weren't even sure where we'd be going from the outset of the ride, so they were discussing various options between themselves and with others on the radio. My client was in the midst of having several realities sink in, including that his partner was dead and that he was facing murder charges as a result, despite not having killed anyone and actually having watched the police apparently do so. Those same police were now taking him to detention, although neither the officers nor we knew exactly where. He was having a panic attack that caused him to hyperventilate and think that he may be having a heart attack, but since the officers would neither take him for medical attention before booking him, nor allow me to physically check him in any way, all I could do was try to lead him through deep breathing exercises while using my voice and eyes to try to bring his focus back to the moment and calm him down with the fact that I was there with him and would remain with him for the duration of the arrest procedure. Following our car was another squad, then the other fellows from my firm, and then a small band of media trucks. Arriving at the former Area 3 headquarters at Belmont and Western, we were initially taken upstairs to the detective division and placed in an interrogation room together, but within minutes we were confronted by several additional officers and a boss who was clearly angered by my presence and who ordered me to wait outside while he verified my identity.

Only after the arrival of my co-counsels and some tense negotiations about why all three of us needed to be there and our refusal to delay our consultation were we allowed back inside with our client. The room had several features that caused us to believe we were being monitored: there was a large pane of mirrored glass, and what appeared to be an electronic installation in the ceiling that certainly wasn't a light and definitely resembled the microphones that were built into some old courthouse tables. We decided to communicate by writing very small notes that we passed back and forth, on which we had written some bluntly direct questions about what exactly happened leading up to the arrival of the police at the apartment. Satisfied that there would not be evidence of drug use or other contraband found during the concurrent searches of our client's apartment, we instructed him very carefully to listen and not speak as we detailed what we knew and advised him what to expect. We kept it brief because we really thought the police were eavesdropping the entire time, and because we insisted they call an ambulance for our client, who had not really managed to regain control of his breathing at any time up to that point. Having served notice on both the client and the police that we were not agreeing to any questioning outside our presence, when the medics took him away, we went back to the office to open a new file and memorialize what we'd seen and done. Sure enough, he later told us that several detectives appeared in his hospital room in the middle of the night to try to get his statement, but despite their pressure, he refused to speak to them. Eventually the autopsy report came back in such a way that he was never charged, and we were never notified of any further police review of the death either. That client was also too scared to complain.

Some people are quick to condemn police abuses as racist, and while there are historical and individual incidents where race is obviously a factor, the issue of institutional failures seems far more complicated than any single cause. Students of logic are taught that even one counterexample can disprove a rule, and there are so many racially diverse officers, and so many racially diverse citizens, that ascribing abuses strictly to racism seems reductive and imprecise. One thing that defense attorneys get asked all the time is "What should I do when the police harass me?" The official answer is a detached fantasy of white America that was barely explained by the US Supreme Court in a case called *Florida v. Bostick*, which is to just ignore the officers and go about your business. I always told my clients: You have to be absolutely clear that you aren't armed. Keep your hands out; make slow movements only. Tell the officers what you are about to do before you do it, like reaching for an insurance card or pulling something out of your pockets. Deciding whether to comply or to object is an academic luxury that usually does not exist on the street. Some things can be undone through legal means, but injuries and death aren't among them.

PDs will tell you of a clear pattern we've seen over the years: there seems to be an unwritten rule in the Chicago Police that anyone who runs away from officers gets beaten if they get caught. It seems to me that the real SOP (standard operating procedure) for the FOP is to train the officers to protect their authority at all costs and without hesitation. Certainly, fleeing felons and anyone with a weapon—or something that could look like a weapon—are in serious danger. We had some clients who were at greater risk of violence than others, and sometimes there would be an opportunity to talk to them about more than just their immediate cases; about their pasts and futures, about their struggles and their anger. In trying to make a point, it can be very easy to be overly dramatic, but there's no need to exaggerate in Chicago: The police will kill you. There will not be an objective investigation. They will probably get away with it. Dead men don't get justice.

XI. REGRETS

The proper mindset for litigation is to be intelligently aggressive. For inspiration, taped to my desk I kept Teddy Roosevelt's quote about the benefits of having a bold disposition that allows for moments of triumph and glory despite the certainty of repeated failure:

> Far better it is to dare mighty things, to win glorious triumphs, even though checkered by failure, than to take rank with those poor spirits who neither enjoy much nor suffer much, because they live in the gray twilight that knows not victory nor defeat.

I'm sure he didn't intend it for public defenders, but it was quite fitting. I also had a painting of a fisherman casting his line into the sea. It wasn't particularly detailed or majestic, and most people who saw it just thought it was a placid seascape, meant to soothe the nerves after a day of courtroom jousting. That watercolor had hung in my childhood room at home. I hadn't chosen it as decoration then, and nobody in my family was into fishing, so in my youth I had no idea why it was there, nor did I attach any special meaning to the image. After law school I found it in storage among other mementos and thought it made a fitting representation of a lone tradesman, standing at the edge of something much larger and more powerful than himself that he needed to regard with the utmost respect but not fear, while using a combination of patient determination and specialized tools to pull out whatever he could from the vast and deadly morass before him.

There are some specific circumstances in criminal defense strategy when there are benefits and even victories to be found in doing nothing, such as when the best option is to remain silent in the face of questioning, or to decline to present a trial defense and instead rest on the failure of the prosecution to meet its burden of proof. However, the majority of cases involve multiple procedural and strategic decisions that require the defense to take affirmative action, each of which must be predicated on a proper calculation of the benefits and risks. As often as I could for major decisions, I ran my ideas by my colleagues and bosses before laying out the situation for my client and seeking their blessing for whatever road I preferred to choose. But many times I found myself on my own, in the heat of the moment, standing at the lectern and facing the judge and the pressure while armed with only my judgment and my willingness to fight. To second-guess is second nature for those whose exercise of judgment has such far-reaching effects on the lives of others. Some of my choices were inevitably wrong; others were probably strategically correct but painful, nonetheless.

Chicago's neighborhoods are notoriously segregated, not entirely by dint of some nefarious plan—although there was plenty of nefarious planning that went into the myriad forms of segregation and exclusionary zoning that stain the history of our city—but also due in part to the inherent nature of immigrant communities wanting to stick together. We have Ukrainian Village, Greek Town, Little Italy, Chinatown, Polish Downtown, and the Mexican enclaves in Pilsen and Little Village. In the late '90s and early 2000s, the Mexican immigrant communities in particular seemed to experience the most influx of new arrivals. For reasons that include financial need, family cohesion, unscrupulous predatory landlords, and, let's just say, EWI realities ("entry without inspection," the legal term for illegal border crossings), I often saw and read police reports about groups of immigrants living together in tightly packed apartments or even garages and storage lockers. Given the nature of our jobs, we didn't see any examples of people who managed to stay out of trouble. What we did see was a large number of cases where people had conflicts in finding or keeping housing or work; using drugs and alcohol to excess and getting into fights; and committing burglaries, robberies, unsophisticated but devastating violence, and sex crimes.

Rape can be charged in many different ways based on the commission of very specific acts as well as other factors like differences in age and the nature of the relationship between alleged perpetrator and victim. Statutes set out numerous charging alternatives, and one common prosecutorial tactic is to charge as many variations as possible, presumably so that there can still be severe convictions where those are justified despite the possibility that one or more counts of an indictment may fail on factually narrow grounds. Where there was once at least a reputation for reluctance to prosecute certain sexual crimes, the pendulum has definitely swung back forcefully in the other direction. Prosecutions in these types of cases now regularly feature indictments with dozens of counts that painstakingly set out each and every separate act of physical contact, forcing any trial into not only very graphic depictions of encounters, but also wearing down defenses and juries with the sheer volume of disgusting prurient detail and the threat of literally centuries behind bars.

The court clerks are the ones who bring the files to the courtroom every morning and organize the call. They and the prosecutors know what's coming. Sheriffs might know too, if they read forms closely enough, since each prisoner arrives with paperwork called a mittimus, where the judges and clerks have written crucial information like court dates and the most important charge against each prisoner. PDs are usually the last ones to find out what surprises await them in the form of new arraignments on any given day. When there are exceptionally severe cases, the clerk and the deputies look at you funny, like you're about to taste something awful and they know it, and they want to watch you throw up.

My worst rape case started with that look. I took my copy of the indictment out of the court file, and the first thing I noticed was that it felt as thick as a magazine. Reading through all the seemingly duplicative counts, I soon realized it was a statutory case, not involving violence or contact between strangers, but apparently a series of encounters between an eighteen-year-old male and an underage girl. For all the rumors and stories that float around about what happens in jail, one of the true unwritten rules is that there are bounties on anyone charged with sex crimes against minors. The sheriffs can decide to treat those defendants with an extra measure of contempt, or just let it be known what they're in for and let the mob do what it will. Some of the courtroom holding areas at 26th Street don't have separate conference rooms, so lawyers have to confer with their clients through the bars while anyone nearby can listen. When there is no privacy, it's practically malpractice to even discuss the charges with your own client because of the compromised privilege and the potential danger. With that kid I remember finding out that he needed an interpreter, so there would be another person who needed to hear the sordid details of whatever we tried to cover in court. I decided to plow through the arraignment without going into too much detail with my client, and I told him I would come to the jail for a private attorney-client conference when we could sit and talk alone.

In a converted laundry room in the basement of Division 1, I learned he was an undocumented immigrant from Mexico who had been living in Chicago for several years. Some distant relatives of his had an apartment that they divided into a sort of shanty hall for various tenants, and he had a space there that was separated from the other residents by sheets that were hung from the ceiling. He worked various menial labor jobs until he landed steady handyman work that kept him busy almost all the time during the weekdays.

When not working, he went to church, played soccer in the park, and, when able, found currency exchanges to wire cash back to Mexico for his parents and siblings. By all accounts I could gather, he avoided trouble with neighborhood gangs and the lure of petty property crimes to augment his modest income and was trying to build a life for himself as best he could, given his illegal entry.

The victim hailed from a traditional, religious, hardworking Mexican family as well, who had also immigrated by unclear means, although by virtue of an amnesty program she was at least a lawful resident. Her parents had a relative who was also on the same path and was also living in the same subdivided labyrinth of laundry in the back room of a two-flat in Humboldt Park. By now I've forgotten the exact details of why she was there; it was either to deliver food or pick up money or paperwork from the relative. She was looking for her cousin and peeled back the wrong sheet and found my client. They both described that first encounter as brief, conversational, and non-private, as there were several others nearby within listening distance. Introductions made and impressions set, he learned the reason for her visit and set in motion the biggest mistake of his life.

He asked how old she was, and she told him she was sixteen. This is significant for three reasons: First, it was a lie. Second, apparently at that time it was entirely socially and legally acceptable in Mexico to date and marry sixteen-year-olds. Third, an objectively reasonable mistake can sometimes, but not always, be used as the basis for a defense in statutory rape cases, and if she was sixteen their relationship would not have been anywhere nearly as illegal as was charged. She supported her assertion by telling him she had graduated from high school, which she had not; by telling him she had a job, which she did not; and with pictures of herself holding the babies of her cousins and telling him she was an aunt, which was also untrue. She appeared fully physically developed in the ways that women do, and told him she was not looking for casual relationships but was fully engaged in the search for a husband. This did not dissuade him, and they began what he thought was a courtship.

Before long, by which I mean within a matter of months, she was pregnant. Again, rather than abandoning her or encouraging an end to the pregnancy, he suggested marriage. When she demurred based on the fear that his proposal was insincere, he persisted and offered to explain everything to her father in the tradition of their culture and religion. However, telling her parents was something she strictly forbade. She was terrified of her father's reaction. That fear led her to hide the pregnancy altogether. She eschewed doctor's visits, prenatal care of any kind, made no changes to her diet or rest, and generally carried on living her life in her usual way. Based on a series of love letters that were exchanged between the two, she was gradually warming to the idea of finding a way to tell her parents about the baby and to getting married and starting a family. She repeatedly assured him that her love was genuine and deep, but that she just needed time to figure out the best way to explain everything to her very traditional family, especially her very strict father.

In the meantime, she began to wear a girdle to hide the growing telltale bump. There were times when her secret was nearly exposed in conversations with her mother or other relatives, but she spun a web of stories that concealed the lovers' rendezvous and the growing biological proof of them. The laws of biology are not as easily dodged as a parent's suspicions, so the emotional strain of her lies and the physical push of her pregnancy against the girdle both built up to the inevitable point where the pressure within exceeded the pressure holding them back, and the girl's fortitude and water both broke, nearly simultaneously. She complained to her mother about unusually strong stomach pains and cramps. Mom apparently thought the symptoms were related to menstruation, and initially gave her daughter an aspirin and sent her to bed. Within minutes, she was jolted into action by terrifying screams emanating from her daughter's room, and arrived to find the girl desperately trying to hide the horrific blood-soaked realities of a medically unsupervised birth in a closet.

After the ambulance transported them to the emergency room and the situation was stabilized, her father arrived and learned the tangled truth. He coordinated with a hospital social worker to call the police, and my client was arrested that very same day while walking home from work, without having any knowledge of the birth, let alone having the chance to talk to the girl or see their baby. During the course of his interrogation, he freely admitted to his relationship with the girl, that he was in love with her, had intercourse with her on at least three occasions, and was the father of their child. Several times he admitted to knowing that she was sixteen and told the officers that they were waiting for her to turn seventeen to announce their wedding plans. He simply had no idea that such a relationship was illegal or wrong. It was only then that the police told him something he could not believe—she was actually only twelve years old, and he was being charged with multiple counts of predatory sexual assault of a child.

The significance of that age is also procedurally crucial: if the alleged victim of a sexual crime is under the age of thirteen in Illinois, it is impossible to use the defense of reasonable mistake. That is, the defendant is legally barred from even trying to claim that he thought she was old enough and have that claim subjected to a test of reasonability that could include facts like her outward appearance, her behavior, her claims of being a certain age, or even her physiological capacity to become pregnant and have a baby. In this case, none of that mattered. If the State could prove that she was twelve and the couple had sex, he was going to be convicted. They had the testimony of her parents, her birth certificate from Mexico, his signed confession, and his DNA in the form of their baby. In the course of the defense investigation, we recovered multiple love letters, the girdle, and found several witnesses to her claims of being sixteen. In fact, the girl was not fully cooperating with the prosecution and had expressed her desire that my client not be charged with such serious crimes. Nothing could convince the State to reduce the charges; the best offer I got from them was ten years in prison, to be followed by immediate deportation upon completion of his sentence.

If we opted for a trial, we had no ability to put on the only defense that was the truth. We would have needed to go to a jury, and if we lost, there was a very high likelihood that he would get a much harsher sentence, something closer to the sixty years that was the top of the range for the charges he was facing. After many difficult conversations with him and explanations of the risks, he took the ten. The charges meant that he was required to serve a minimum of 85 percent, or eight and a half years, since there are several categories of crimes for which prisoners are not eligible for the standard day-for-day credits, and his convictions were in that category.

At the sentencing hearing, I brought two interpreters—the one that was required for him to understand the proceedings, and another one to read the love letters the girl had written to him into the record while she and her parents stood there listening to every word. It took about ten minutes to read each one aloud, and during that time I thought I could feel the mood of the judge and the entire courtroom staff change dramatically from being ready to absolutely crucify him to at least a shred of understanding. I shudder to think what it must have been like for him to be in maximum security on a conviction for child rape, without the ability to explain the context or details, and probably nobody really caring to hear them anyway. I imagine it was very hard time to do. I will always harbor a stone of regret for not taking his case to trial and challenging the authenticity of her Mexican birth certificate with some argument that those documents can be easily forged, which her parents were more than willing to do in order to prevent the marriage between their daughter and a kid they considered unworthy. If we could have combined that argument with the defense of reasonable mistaken age based on what she had said and what her body was clearly capable of doing, we might've won. I'll never know, but they weren't years of my life with which I would have had to gamble. For ten full years after the day we entered that plea, I regularly checked the calendar, wondering how my client was doing, hoping he was able to survive prison, praying he would rebuild his life upon release. I was hoping I'd feel better when the ten years were over, but I absolutely do not.

Not all my professional regrets concern losses. Despite being relatively far from downtown and the nightspots of its closer neighborhoods like Wicker Park or Lincoln Park, the Broadway corridor at its intersection with Lawrence Avenue sees plenty of weekend action thanks to attractions like the Green Mill Tavern, concerts at the Riviera Theatre and the Aragon Ballroom, and the Red Line train stop that serves them all. The area is very well lit and heavily trafficked, but the urban bustle can provide a cloak of anonymity, and the natural ebb and flow of the architecture combined with the numerous and varied obstructions of the city form slices of shadow and shards of darkness among the glitter. There is a large triangular lot at the intersection that for a long time has housed at least one bank, with a set of ATMs located at the back of the building in the parking lot, set off at a significant distance from the street. That seclusion, along with the clunking screech of the train and maybe a broken streetlight or two, creates the perfect opportunity for darkness of another kind.

On one particular jaunty evening on the North Side, a young woman in her mid-twenties felt safe enough to take brief leave of her friends as they were on their way to one of the area attractions and headed for those backlot ATMs. There is no poetry in being mugged, an experience to which too many can relate. As her cash slid out of the machine slot, a large man grabbed her from behind in such a way that confused her about whether she was being robbed or raped or both, since her blouse was torn as he spun her around to demand the money she'd just withdrawn. The remnants of her top slid down to her elbows as he thrashed her. His haul was exactly sixty bucks. After he ran off toward the train station, she clasped the shreds of her clothes together and ran to find her friends.

A good Samaritan saw the disheveled victim with a frantic look about her, clad in a bra and strips of a shirt, and offered her the use of his cell phone and the refuge of his car. The police were on the scene within two or three minutes and took down a profile that was enough to begin a search of the area, but bore the typical generic quality of so many quick descriptions: black male, approximately five foot ten, medium build, short hair, wearing jeans and a white or off-white jacket. When I was reading the police reports for this case, it instantly triggered memories of a long-rumored CPD order that was supposedly used by sergeants when a particular set of circumstances called for swift old-fashioned roundups in the fresh aftermath of violent street crimes: "Bring me two tons of nigger and we'll figure it out from there."

Tactical and patrol squads fanned out to canvass the area as quickly as possible, trying to locate suspects in the immediate vicinity before there was time for the perpetrator to get too far away. A pair of officers went into a bar less than two blocks from the scene and immediately spotted someone matching most of the description, except he had a white shirt instead of a jacket. They placed him in their car and arranged a drive-by viewing called a show-up (instead of a lineup, where there is more than one person to choose from). The victim was given a chance to identify him as he sat in the back of a squad car while they shone powerful lights in his face that would prevent him from seeing her. Behind the glare of the lights and from whatever distance separated her and the car, she said it was him and they bundled him off to the district for booking. The proceeds weren't recovered and neither was any weapon, but the total time between the incident and the identification was around fifteen minutes, so there was enough confidence for the ASA on Felony Review to approve the charges.

My client was a frequent flier looking at Class X time based on his background, meaning mandatory pen with a six-year floor and a thirty-year ceiling. Street slang for committing a robbery is called "hitting a lick," and this would not have been his first one. Given his sheet, he was a bit older than typical robbery defendants, who are usually very young. If there is such a thing as a professional defendant, this guy was it: stoic, calm, all-business in the lockup and before the bench. We worked together as cleanly as we could and arrived at a mutual agreement that we'd take it to a jury, with the defense being the classic lack of proof, hinting at "SODDI" (some other dude did it).

Sometimes the State comes up with a fire-sale offer if their victim doesn't feel up to the task of testifying, but this woman was solid as a rock. We pecked away with the usual line of "poor opportunity to observe" since it was a shocking event that was very brief and had occurred between interracial strangers. We made some hay out of the slightly mismatched clothing description; the fact that the prosecution didn't bring anyone from the bar to say he'd run in shortly before he was dragged out; the lack of matching cash on him; the suggestive nature of the show-up; and our best point, which was that in his booking photos he had a wispy beard that the victim never mentioned in giving her description. But she never broke under cross, and even doubled down on her certainty by mentioning his eyes. She said she couldn't forget the unusually light coloring of his eyes as he glared at her fear in the heat of the moment. He didn't testify. Throughout the closing arguments, I don't think he so much as even fidgeted in his chair.

After about an hour of deliberations, the jury sent out a request asking to see the booking photos, and the judge asked both sides for any objections. The State had none, but I did, arguing that sending back the booking photo was tantamount to another lineup of one that had no practical purpose beyond improper suggestion of guilt. The judge overruled me in about two seconds flat and had the sheriff take the originals back to the jury room. To be honest, I was bracing for a quick defeat after that, thinking that his oddly colored eyes would tip the scale. I confessed as much to the judge during the time he ordered pizza for all the courtroom staff while we were waiting for a verdict.

Evening hours at Cook County courthouses are quiet times, in stark contrast to the hum of daily business. It has the feel of staying long after school, with free run of the building and an opportunity for bonding with the people who spend each day as adversaries. The hours tick by, and the lawyers sit together wondering what in the world could possibly be taking so long. We have a chance to tour the State's Attorney's Office, looking at their giddy collection of cut-off neckties that serve as trophies from the first jury win for whoever was wearing them at the time. They can come by our offices, too, and laugh at the closet full of hobo clothes we stock for defendant dress-up. Eventually, the phone rings with the courtroom clerk on the other end, and we take that nerve-racking walk back down to the courtroom to learn our client's fate.

Normally there is plenty of joy in getting a "Not Guilty." When the foreperson reads the sheet and says those magic words, there is immense professional vindication, and the absolutely intoxicating feeling of knowing that a person is regaining their freedom thanks to your months of effort and steely counsel. Gathering my composure, I had a moment to lean over to my client in a celebratory half-hug, expecting some exasperated relief on his part, but there was nothing from him. Again, he barely registered an acknowledgment. On the other hand, the victim, who was sitting in the second row of the gallery to hear the outcome, burst into sobs and shrieks of disbelief. Her reaction was raw, incredulous, and clearly very pained, along the lines of a panic attack. The lead prosecutor dashed to her side and whispered something in her ear, cradling her shoulder as she guided her out of the courtroom. The sheriffs whisked my client down the elevator, and I never spoke to him again. Polling the jury and talking to them afterward, they said they'd found reasonable doubt in the fact that the victim failed to mention the beard. The judge headed back with them to thank them for their service, sign their certificates, and have a final word.

I waited in the courtroom for him to come back and critique my performance. Actually, in addition to his tutorial, I was waiting for a chance to gloat about my strategic prowess in using a strike on a potential juror during jury selection that the judge had criticized along the way. There was a young woman in the jury pool who had no obvious flaws, but whom I suspected would identify with the victim too easily and may be emotionally swayed. The judge had lectured my approach that he considered too picky: "You don't *select* a jury, you *de-select* a jury." Having suitably admitted I was right and he was impressed, he took a swipe back by letting me know he'd told the jury about my objection to them examining the booking photo as he dismissed them. Having confessed that I was really afraid they'd look into the defendant's eyes and see the same thing the victim did, I muttered something about the judge selling me down the river, which he was positively gleeful to confirm. When the prosecutor rejoined the postmortem, I asked her what she'd said to console the victim. The prosecutor was a woman with a lot of experience and such a solemn demeanor that none of us were used to seeing her get emotional. She cast her eyes downward and took a deep breath, and said, "I just told her that it wasn't her fault."

Long before I ever got to felony court, I was working a misdemeanor retail theft call from the suburbs, which was always incredibly frustrating because it involved watching wannabe rent-a-cops pretend to be justice warriors as they diligently worked to lock up people who were desperate enough to attempt to walk out of a multi-tiered loss prevention system with diapers or formula or clothing that amounted to absolutely nothing for the massive retail chains who pretended to be the victims. Retail theft up to a value of $150 was a misdemeanor, but anything above that was a felony. Under certain circumstances, the misdemeanors could be resolved with an order of supervision instead of probation, allowing the defendants to meet various rehabilitative conditions and have their records wiped clean as if nothing ever happened.

As usual, there was a catch that prevented defendants from being eligible for supervision if they were charged under a particular subsection that alleged they had harmed the store security agent during the course of their arrest. Even that could usually be circumvented with a certain amount of nagging, as long as the case facts weren't particularly egregious and the prosecutor shared a sense that the loss prevention agent was being a bit dramatic. However, there were times when an ASA would say that he or she couldn't reduce one of those due to pressure from the store, but would allow us on the defense to try to get the reduction from the judge in a plea conference that would be held out of the watchful eye of the store rep. When that happened to me for the first time as I was feeling my way through the contours of the system in my early years, I was simultaneously frustrated by the inflexibility of the prosecutor and eager to prove to the judge that I wasn't ignorant of the implications of the different statutory sections. As I stood up to request the conference, I gave a thorough explanation on the record of the impasse in our plea negotiations and the need for the judge to step in and consider the reduction that I thought was fitting.

Normally plea conferences are set aside to accumulate in a group as the call progresses, allowing for more basic matters like continuances to be settled before the judge takes time off the bench to hear plea proposals and consider formal offers. The routine of the conferences also includes the attendance of both prosecution and defense in chambers, lest there be any suggestion of improper *ex parte* communications. I was too young and naive to suspect anything amiss when the judge accepted my request for such a meeting and interrupted the call to hold it right away. Maybe I should've realized as we cleared the risers behind the bench and entered the back hallway, when the judge turned to tell the ASA that he wanted a minute with me alone before the others who would be joining made their way in; but no, I charged ahead with the feeling that I was being given a special audience.

Judges are always guarded at work, but they each have a more relaxed persona than the image they project from the bench. Depending on the type of break or working recess the judge needs, they might take the opportunity to throttle down into a different mode, and pour themselves a drink or grab a snack. This judge had a well-known habit of smoking a cigarette at almost every opportunity, and true to form, he kept his back to me as we entered his chambers and told me to close the door behind myself. He headed for the tobacco box behind his desk, which seemed perfectly normal. I remember the dawning surprise I felt as he first lit up that cigarette, then immediately turned around and lit into me. Huffing and puffing with nicotine and disgust, he patronizingly explained that even if he wanted to help me, I had made it impossible due to my courtroom babbling. He told me that if he did as I was asking, he would have to be the one to force the State to reduce the charges, and he had no interest in a public reputation for that kind of lenience. He lectured, "Son, you have to learn how things are done around here." Then he stressed: *"Never educate the public."*

I suppose there was value in a blunt Chicago lesson about how to work behind closed doors, but my job was literally defending the public, and telling the truth about what goes into our work feels like a vital part of it.

I only wish that I could have been better; that I could have done more.

ACKNOWLEDGMENTS

I wish to extend my utmost gratitude to the dedicated professionals who helped in the publication of this book, most notably Timothy Mennel and the staff at the University of Chicago Press, and Professor Bill Savage at Northwestern University; and my deepest respect to all the past, present, and future public defenders across America, who are the overworked, underpaid, and vastly underappreciated guardians of liberty on behalf of those who need it most. In particular, to the men and women with whom I had the honor of working in Cook County District 2 Skokie: Gino, Mark, Frank, Camille, Wendy, Deanna, Henry, Tony, Geoff, Howard, Susan, Audruy, Jeannie, Bob G., Bob M., John P., Owen, Andy, Elly, Gerry, Hilary, Jan, Gayle, Janine, Audrey, Mike M., Bruce, Tom, Faye, Mike B., Anita, Mary, Helen, Dolores, Heather, Dawn, Tanya, and, of course, Ralph.

INDEX

Firearm Owner's Identification Card (FOID), 54
first chair, 52, 58, 60
first responders, 14, 19, 182
Florida v. Bostick, 195
Ford Heights Four, 175
Forensic Science Division, 57, 80
Four Corner Hustlers, 155
Fox, Kevin, 77, 79; interrogation of, as coercive manipulation, 78
Fox, Riley, 76–79
Fraternal Order of Police (FOP), 182, 190, 195
Freeman, Jack, 30
"frequent fliers," 3, 17, 50, 206

game theory, 13
Garland, Merrick, 67
gaslighting, 4
Gauger, Gary, 175
Girl X, 22–23, 27
Goldston Report, 178
gravitas, 47, 75
Greylord scandal, 70–71, 81
Guevara, Reynaldo, 179–80
Gulf War Syndrome (GWS), 97
gun control, 114
gun crimes, 103–24; felony enhancements, 98; gun manufacturers, 125; gunshot residue (GSR), 80
gun ownership, 113; for protection, 115–16; self-defense, 115
gun possession, 53–54, 97–98, 100, 103, 108, 114

Haggerty, LaTanya, 25
Hammond, Big John, 184; Officer Friendly, 183
Hampton, Fred, 120–22
Harold L. Ickes Homes, 161
Hastert, Dennis, 110

Health Insurance Portability and Accountability Act (HIPAA), 135
"heater cases"/"heaters," 45, 61, 80, 96, 105, 188
Heineman, Ben, Jr., 117–18
Hernandez, Alejandro, 72–73, 174
Herrera, Keith, 159
Hicks, Eddie, 157, 160
Highland Park, IL, 114
Hobbs, Jerry, 75–76
Hobbs, Laura, 75–76
Hobos (street gang), 161
Hoffa, Jimmy, 29
Holiday Bond Court, 2–3, 12
Hometown, IL, 29
Homicide Task Force, 40, 57–58, 171
Hoover, J. Edgar, 121
horizontal overcharging, 86–87
Horwich, Theodore, 28, 30–31
Hull House, 37

Ida B. Wells Homes, 160–61
Illinois, xiii, 1, 71–72, 79, 115, 202; clout in, 75; death penalty, troubled history of, 173, 176–77; Death Row, 174–75, 178; illegal gun possession, 97–98; police agencies, 181
Illinois Black Panther Party, 120–22
Illinois Department of Corrections (IDOC): 61 days for a year in prison, 86
Illinois Secretary of State Police, 181
Illinois State Police, 163–64, 181–82; Bureau of Identification, 92; crime lab, 72, 77, 150
Illinois Supreme Court: Capital Litigation Trial Bar, 57; Rule 711, 103, 106
incarceration, 88, 91, 169; freedom, difference between, 43; mass, xii; privatized, 34; urban, 16